MORE THAN WORDS

MORE THAN WORDS

William Sydnor

1817

Harper & Row, Publishers, San Francisco

New York, Grand Rapids, Philadelphia, St. Louis
London, Singapore, Sydney, Tokyo, Toronto

To Eleanor Sandt (1903–1987)
Colleague of yesteryear and,
by the grace of God, my friend

Library of Congress Cataloging-in-Publication Data

Sydnor, William.
   More than words / William Sydnor. — 1st ed.
     p.   cm.
   Includes bibliographical references.
   ISBN 0-06-067778-3
   1. Theology—Dictionaries. I. Title.
   BR95.S93   1990   89-46023
   203—dc20   CIP

90 91 92 93 94 HAD 10 9 8 7 6 5 4 3 2

This edition is printed on acid-free paper which meets the American
National Standards Institute Z39.48 Standard.

CONTENTS

PREFACE

This book is intended to be a helpful tool for leaders, teachers, clergy, and ordinary Bible readers who need a ready reference to the meaning of the much-used words of the Christian's vocabulary. It is a keep-it-at-your-elbow book for such people regardless of denomination.

This book is also intended to be used as a stepping stone to deepening faith. Those just beginning to learn about Christianity need a source to which they can turn in their effort to understand it better. And certainly those beginning a new chapter of seriousness in the faith—such as the newly confirmed—want a source to which they can turn when there is a question of more than dictionary dimensions. Christians already quite familiar with the faith know that the meanings of familiar words sometimes become covered with the dust of vagueness and need to be polished up a bit—made shiny again and refilled with meaning. *More Than Words* is intended to offer insight to Christians on each of these levels of faith.

A book like this is full of borrowed ideas. In this case even the title is borrowed from a book more than three decades old.

In the 1950s the Episcopal Church published a new series of graded Sunday school materials under the title the Seabury Series. In addition to a teacher's manual for each grade, there was also a student resource book. The seventh grade student book was called *More Than Words* and was a book of descriptive definitions of 108 words which were likely to come up in class discussions. The book first appeared in 1955, was revised in 1958, then went out of print. However, some teachers held on to their copies of *More Than Words* and used them as *their own* reference book—a treasured possession.

This book is an expanded *More Than Words*, addressing the need the former student book was inadequately meeting in its last days. It builds on the idea of the original student book, but there the likeness ceases. It further seeks to throw light on the meaning of more than two hundred words which the people mentioned above come across continually, and for which they would like a ready source of reference.

Of course, many persons and books have contributed to the insights I have tried to set forth simply and clearly in these definitions. The Reverend Doctor Charles P. Price, sometime professor of Systematic Theology, Virginia Theological Seminary, Alexandria, Virginia, is at the head of that list. But of course, he cannot be blamed for any of my errors in interpretation.

The spirit of the original *More Than Words* is a legacy from Eleanor E. Sandt, its Seabury Series editor. These words from the preface of the 1958 edition express it:

> This book makes no effort to convince anyone of any of the lesser points about which church people differ. Its purpose is to present clearly the important things on which we agree.

That is what I have tried to do also. And, if I have succeeded, *laus Deo.*

William Sydnor

A

Absolution

ABSOLUTION is a church word that means setting free from sin. It is God's pardon spoken by the minister or priest. In the practice of the Hebrew Temple the priest had a sort of representative role. The Hebrews were a graphic-minded people. The priest entered the sanctuary and offered the people's prayers which went up to God in the smoke of the incense. Then he returned to bless the people in God's name and to pronounce God's absolution of their sins. He was their representative before God and God's representative before them.

It is true that every one of us has direct access to God, a point which the Protestant Reformation stressed. Yet when we have sinned we become outsiders. We have separated ourselves from God and from the family of his people, the Church. We long to be taken back into the family. The words a minister or priest uses to bring us back are called "absolution." When spoken, the words are spoken representatively for God and for all God's people. God and his Church are taking us, penitent and forgiven sinners, back in good standing.

This is somewhat similar to what happens in our families. A member of the family "goes away mad" and mother succeeds in bringing him back. When she puts her arm around him and forgives him, she is doing it, not just for herself but for the whole family. She says the words, but the whole family forgives him. In God's family the ordained person up front says the words, but the forgiveness comes from God and from his Church.

Absolution is sometimes individual—the penitent and the pastor or priest alone. At other times it is done in a public service—all of us are guilty together, have a need to confess, and to receive forgiveness. Communities and nations sin, so all of us, individually and corporately, need to be absolved, taken back into the supportive fellowship of God's family wherein we find the strength to live and serve more faithfully.

See Confession, Forgiveness, Reconciliation.

Adoption

ADOPTION is the act of taking someone in and making him or her a full-fledged member of the family. In the New Testament the term is used by Paul to describe our relationship to the Heavenly Father through our faith in Jesus Christ.

We know about this change of status in family relationships. Christian missionaries living in Nepal take an orphan Nepalese baby into their home and make her a member of their family, both emotionally and legally. The baby is an outsider; then through the adoption of love and law she acquires a wonderful new status. She now belongs to a family; she is included, cared about (and cared for), and loved. She is secure.

Paul explains our relationship to God in similar terms. Because of sin—our willfulness and self-centeredness—the normal relationship God intended for us has been broken. We are "orphans," separated from our Heavenly Father. But God wants us back in spite of our sin; so he sent his Son into the world to rescue us from the power of sin, that we might become his adopted children:

> God sent forth his Son, born of a woman, . . . so that we might receive the adoption of sons. And because you are sons, God has sent the Spirit of his Son into our hearts, crying, "Abba! [meaning] Father!" (Gal. 4:4-6)

We are "made God's children by adoption and grace" (Rom. 8:15; Eph. 1:5-7, KJV), as an ancient prayer puts it.

Adoration

ADORATION is that kind of prayer in which we tell God, "I love you," simply because he is God. There are no strings attached. Johnny loves Mary; "I adore you," he says. Johnny is content just to be with her. He is not asking for anything, explaining anything; they just want to be with each other. If there are words, they are "sweet nothings."

Our prayers of adoration have something of that quality. "Holy, holy, holy Lord, God of power and might, heaven and earth are full of your glory!" This is beyond praise. It has a quality of awesome wonder. We are his creatures; he is God "before whom angels veil their faces," and *he loves us*. Ours is a responding love.

This does not mean that we understand everything he does, or even like everything he does. How many lovers understand (or even like) everything their beloved does? That does not matter. We know enough to be awed; we stand in speechless wonder before God.

Francis of Assisi is said to have prayed, "O God, help me to *want* to love you." If you *want* to love God, then you have expressed the deepest utterance of the human heart. This is the response of adoration.

All true prayer is worship—ascribing worth to the Eternal God. Without adoration, thanksgiving may become miserliness, petition a selfish clamor, intercession a currying of special favors for our friends, and even confession may turn into a refined indulgence. The "Hallelujah Chorus" lifts us out of the bog of our pettiness and sets our feet on the high ground of adoration.

Adoration is the highest form of prayer.

See Prayer.

Advocate

AN ADVOCATE is one who pleads another's case, an intercessor, a defender. The word is used in the New Testament to refer to Christ. "If anyone sins, we have an advocate with the Father, Jesus Christ the righteous; and he is the expiation for our sins, and not for ours only but also for the sins of the whole world" (1 John 2:1).

This is one of the ways in which the early Christians tried to put into words their conviction that Jesus Christ has saved those who put their faith in him from the eternal consequences of their sins. It is a legal turn of phrase. He both pleads our case—as our "Advocate with the Father"—and by his Passion and death he is the expiation (the one who makes amends) for our sins.

In Greek, the same word for "advocate" is also used to speak of the Holy Spirit (John 14:16, 26). Transliterated into English it is "Paraclete." When it is used to refer to the Spirit it is often translated "Counselor" or "Comforter." Thus our Lord continues to defend and support us through the Holy Spirit, the Counselor, who will be with us forever (John 14:16).

See Atonement, Holy Spirit.

Almighty

ALMIGHTY refers to the invincible power of God. We usually think of power as physical force, but when trying to describe the omnipotence of God we are thinking of moral and spiritual power. His sovereign will cannot ultimately be thwarted.

In Jesus we see the almightiness, the invincible power of divine love. We see him reaching out in love and mercy and compassion to despised tax-collectors, prostitutes, lepers, beggars—the nobodies of society. Then, when his life is reaching its climax, he is betrayed, deserted, maligned, cruelly treated, and barbarously put to death. And yet his love for people never wavers. He prays, "Father, forgive them," and reaches out in love to the penitent thief and to his sorrowing mother. The Crucifixion scene is a striking picture of undaunted love, all-powerful love. Years after it took place Paul wrote, "Nothing can separate us from the love of God in Christ Jesus our Lord" (Rom. 8:39). This is divine almightiness. Nothing can overcome it; nothing can destroy it. The Passion of our Lord demonstrates that all the concerted forces of evil—lying, arrogance, hatred, avarice, cowardice, selfishness, and the rest—cannot overpower the love of God in Christ. Sin did its worst: it killed him. But God raised him from the dead. Even death is powerless before the almighty love of God.

Alms/Offering

ALMS are our contributions and gifts which support the Church and its work. Contributions of food are given to the poor. Contributions of money (usually known as "the offering") are used to fund the local church and its ministries at home and abroad. An offertory anthem or hymn is often sung while the offering is being collected.

Our offerings are considerably more than contributions toward the church's upkeep, downspouts, and outreach. The money we put in the offering plate can have a significant spiritual dimension. At the offertory, we are presenting to the Lord not just dollars but a portion of our dedicated selves. Our dollars are what we can materially show for the hours and days of our creative existence. If, for example, I am paid ten dollars an hour for the work I do at my nine-to-five job, then ten dollars represents one hour of my creative existence, one hour of my life during which I was using the abilities God has given me. I come to church and in gratitude for God's goodness to me I give back to him a portion of life – of my creative ability in a negotiable, transportable form – so that it can be translated into service in his Name, perhaps in some distant place.

There was once a store clerk who yearned to respond to the Lord's command to Christians to "go ye into all the world . . . teaching them to observe all that I have commanded you." But she could not; she had to stay in Toledo and take care of her aged mother. However, she would not be defeated. Every week she spent a day imagining herself teaching in a school in Liberia or a prison in Texas, or to slum children in New York City. The following Sunday her offering was the monies she had earned on her missionary day clerking in a store.

For such a person the presentation of the offertory as part of Sunday's service can be an exciting moment.

Amen

AMEN is an expression of approval or agreement. It is a Hebrew word which has been taken over into English. Amen, as the concluding response at the end of prayers, might be translated "So be it" or "That's how I feel." The King James Version of the Bible translates it "verily," which means "truly." The Chinese have no character for the word *amen*. They use the rather engaging expression, "That is my heart's desire."

Angels

ANGELS are God's messengers who praise him in heaven and assist him on earth.

The Bible contains many references to angels appearing to warn people, to guide them, or to inform them. An angel prepared Elijah for a difficult journey when he was fleeing from Queen Jezebel's wrath (1 Kings 19:1-8). The angel Gabriel told Mary that she would be the mother of our Lord (Luke 1:26-31). A host of angels appeared to the shepherds in the Christmas story (Luke 2:13-14). An angel rescued Peter from prison (Acts 12:6–11). Sometimes the angel messenger is God himself (Gen. 18:1–12; 19:1–2).

The Bible makes it clear that God has messengers and helpers besides human people. These heavenly messengers still speak to us, warning us of evil and encouraging us to do good. We acknowledge their presence, perhaps, without realizing it. We say, "I had a hunch everything was going to turn out all right," or "I don't know where I ever found the courage." At a high point in the Eucharist in the Episcopal church human praise is united with that of the angelic host: "Therefore we praise you joining our voices with angels and archangels, and with all the company of heaven."

The secret of sleight-of-hand magic is that as a rule people see only what they expect to see. Frederick Buechner says that since we do not expect to see angels, we don't. Maybe he's right.

Anointing

ANOINTING WITH OIL has been part of Christian ceremonies since early times, having deep Old Testament roots. Oil was used to set apart certain people as special; kings were anointed to set them apart as sacred for their high calling (1 Sam. 16:13), as were priests (Lev. 4:5). It was a Jewish practice to anoint the body with oil after bathing. So it is not surprising that anointing with oil slipped into Christian baptism, a spiritual washing, as early as the first century.

Because oil signifies richness, abundance, and healing, it was a natural symbol of the fullness of divine life whose source was the Christ which literally means the "Anointed One." When one was healed and strengthened by anointing with oil, it was Christ who communicated his strength and compassion to the sick person.

Scholars generally agree that baptism in New Testament times included being anointed with oil although the actual words are not to be found. It was a symbol that the person was sealed with the Holy Spirit (2 Cor. 1:22; Eph. 1:13; 1 John 2:20, 27).

Chrism is the consecrated oil used in baptism. It is the "seal"; using the oil to mark the candidate's forehead with the sign of the cross symbolizes the fact he or she is sealed by the Holy Spirit when baptized, and marked as Christ's own (Eph. 4:30).

See Baptism, Christ.

Antichrist

ANTICHRIST is the name applied to that person (or group) who is absolutely opposed to Christ. There have been a variety of opponents of Christ who have been thought of in this way.

In the New Testament there is reference to him "who denies that Jesus is the Christ" and thus sought to deceive the faithful (1 John 2:22).

Down through the ages Antichrist has often been identified with the oppressive political power of the time—Nero, Napoleon, Bismarck, Hitler. At other times "the great deceiver" has been thought of as an ecclesiastical power: Wycliffe and Luther held that the papacy was Antichrist, and more recently ecclesiastical splinter groups have looked upon the World Council of Churches in this way.

In every case Antichrist has been thought of as fighting against the redemptive word of Christ and his Church.

Apocalypse

APOCALYPSE literally means to uncover or reveal. Apocalypse initially referred to Jewish or Christian writings during the period 200 B.C. through A.D. 350 that were assumed to reveal God's ultimate purpose. The Apocalypse of John the Divine, commonly called the Book of Revelation, is the best known of these writings. Christian apocalyptic thought and writing has to do with the end of the world, the return of Christ, and the Last Judgment, and it forecasts imminent disaster and universal destruction. The prospect of nuclear war gives rise to apocalyptic thinking and writing in our own time.

Apocrypha

THE APOCRYPHA is a term used to denote several texts found in some early Christian versions of the Old Testament, but not given full canonical status today (meaning that they are not included in some canons of the Bible). The apocryphal books which are found in the Septuagint (the Greek version of the Old Testament) are:

Additions to Esther
Baruch

Bel and the Dragon

The First and Second Books of Esdras

Judith

The Letter of Jeremiah

The First, Second, Third, and Fourth Books of the Maccabees

The Prayer of Manasseh

Psalm 151

Eccelsiasticus

The Prayer of Azariah and the Song of the Three Young Men

Susanna

Tobit

The Wisdom of Solomon

The majority of these texts are found in Roman Catholic and/or Eastern Orthodox canons of the Old Testament. The books of the Apocrypha are not considered authoritative by most Protestant churches; while parts of some of them are read in some Protestant churches there are reservations. The "Articles of Religion," an Episcopal document dating from 1801 (*Book of Common Prayer*, p. 868), gently describes their sphere of influences: "The Church doth read them for example of life and instruction of manners; but yet doth not apply them to establish any doctrine."

See Bible.

Apostle

AN APOSTLE is a person who is sent forth in Christ's name. An apostle is sent with authority, having been given a message to carry to someone else. Today when ambassadors are appointed and sent to some foreign country, they speak and act with the authority which has been given them.

In the New Testament we read that our Lord chose twelve men to be with him. (The writers of the first three Gospels—Matthew, Mark, and Luke—give us slightly different lists of the twelve appointed by Jesus. John's Gospel mentions only eight.) Jesus called them to be his disciples or pupils. Later he sent them out to preach the Good News of the Kingdom of God, to drive out demons, and to heal. The twelve whom Jesus chose came to be called *apostles*. They had been given authority and power to act in the Name of Jesus. They had learned from Jesus, had shared his life, and had seen his work. Later they were witnesses of his Resurrection.

When Judas Iscariot, one of the twelve, betrayed Jesus, and then committed suicide, the remaining eleven men met and chose a twelfth man, Matthias, to take Judas' place (Acts 1:15–26). This story gives the qualifications of an apostle: he must have been with Jesus throughout his ministry and must have been a witness to the Resurrection. Later on, Paul, Barnabas, and others were also considered apostles (Acts 13:1–3).

There is a difference between an apostle and a disciple. A disciple is a learner who is loyal to his teacher. An apostle has Christ's authority to teach and to act in his Name. The Risen Christ appeared to the eleven and said,

> Go therefore and make disciples of all nations, baptizing them in the name of the Father and of the Son and of the Holy Spirit, teaching them to observe all that I have commanded you, and lo, I am with you always, to the close of the age. (Matt. 28:19–20)

The disciples then became apostles.

See Disciple.

Apostolic Succession

APOSTOLIC SUCCESSION is the line of succession from the apostles to the present through the bishops of the Church. It is considered an important link of present ecclesiastical authority with that of the apostles of our Lord, an authority which is passed on through ordination to the bishops and clergy of each succeeding generation.

This belief and practice is intended to ensure the authenticity of the Church's orders and sacraments. It is considered especially important by Roman, Eastern Orthodox, and Anglican churches, assuring the validity of their ministries and the authority of their teachings.

There is both a profound truth and a serious problem here. The great truth is that in the Gospel accounts the apostles are the primary witnesses to the Lord's Resurrection. The Church rightly wants to maintain its direct relation to that vital past. Apostolic succession has a sort of sacramental quality. It is the outward and visible sign of an inward and spiritual grace—the grace that is ours because we belong to that great company of believers in the Resurrection from New Testament times right down to today. The problem related to apostolic succession is raised by historically minded folk who often take a dim view of this belief because there are shady areas in the early centuries of the Christian church where historical records and historical accuracy are very hard to come by or even nonexistent. But the belief does not thereby crumble, for it is not based on mechanics. Rather, it is borne witness to by the determination of the Church in every succeeding generation to "continue in the apostles' teaching and fellowship" (Acts 2:42). This is symbolically demonstrated by having the bishops—the designated custodians of the faith—receive their commission (which is what ordination means) from their predecessors, and then, in turn, pass it on to their successors.

An easily available document that bears witness to this belief is the hymnal in the pews of our churches. For example, the origin the words of the songs of prayer and praise in *The Hymnal 1982* of the Episcopal church reveal origins from every century of the Christian era, from New Testament times to the present. So not only is a continuous succession of custodians of the faith a symbol of the apostolic belief handed down to us from the earliest days, the hymns we sing bear that same witness.

Asceticism

ASCETICISM is a solitary, contemplative mode of life in which there is a self-discipline of rigorous abstinence from indulgence in pleasure by celibacy, fasting, and self-mortification. Basically, it is an attempt to flee the present. The ascetic is seeking to live in the past or in the future. Pagan ascetics looked to the past. But the past is a dead end; to put it on a pedestal is idolatry. On the other hand, when the past is treated as a stepping stone it can be an element in our preparation for the future. The Christian ascetic looks to the future, and prepares him or herself in anticipation of the coming Kingdom of God. Of the Essenes, that ancient monastic community which left us the Dead Sea Scrolls, scholars say, "The life of the sect is understood as life in anticipation of the Kingdom of God" (*The Interpreter's Bible*, vol. 12, 1957, p. 666).

The ascetic is a strange person to many Christians, especially Protestants. What is the point of weeks and even months of never saying a word, of a rough hair shirt, of hours of incessant prayer, of endless long periods of extreme fasting. And celibacy. The Bible certainly enjoins us to train for the spiritual life, discipline our bodies and our desires. But the non-ascetic says, "I have a family, a job, everyday responsibilities. Does Christian spirituality have to be that extreme?"

No. Every Christian does not have the vocation to be an ascetic. Indeed, only a comparatively few have such a vocation. But in the long life of the Church the ascetics have made an inestimable contribution to which all denominations of the Church are indebted.

We are indeed thankful for the liberations of the Renaissance and the Reformation from certain asceticisms of the Middle Ages. The liberty of the Christian individual was rediscovered in that sixteenth century by the Reformers, truly a precious good. But turn back the centuries. In the Roman civilization of New Testament times and after, sexual immorality had gone to bestial extremes. "It is a shame even to speak of the things that they do in secret" (Eph. 5:12). Some dedicated Christians fled from the wickedness which they witnessed everywhere. These people, who are our ancestors in the faith, went into caves, into the desert, or undertook monastic disciplines in their revolt against pagan Rome. As T.O. Wedel put it, "There is a human filthiness which goes not out but by fasting and prayer" (*The Interpreter's Bible*, vol. 10, 1953, p. 706).

It is true that there were some orgies of asceticism and the result has been adverse. St. Francis frankly confessed that "his austerities made him irritable, querulous, bad-tempered, less Christlike than he would have been under a saner scheme of life" (*The Interpreter's Bible*, vol. 8, 1952, p. 683). However, there is no telling what prevalent distortions of ancient times might have seeped into the mainstream of Christian faith and practice had it not been for the awesome dedication of the ancient ascetics.

Atonement

ATONEMENT is the act of making amends so that estranged persons can be at one again. I make amends for my surly unneighborliness toward the fellow next door by helping his little daughter find her lost puppy or by cleaning the snow off his walk. We become friends again. "At-one-ment" has taken place.

Our sins have created a barrier between us and our Heavenly Father, a barrier so great that we cannot possibly remove it. God in his love takes the initiative. He sends his Son into the world, who by his life and suffering and death removes that barrier caused by our sin. We are forgiven, taken back as his penitent and pardoned children, and become heirs of eternal life.

This divine act is couched in a variety of biblical expressions. Here are two of them:

> By his stripes we are healed. . . .
> and the Lord has laid on him
> the iniquity of us all. (Isa. 53:5–6)

> In this is love, not that we loved God, but that he loved us
> and sent his Son to be the expiation for our sins. (1 John 4:10)

Let us think of atonement as removing those obstacles which block the possibility of a happy relationship between Creator and creature, making it possible for our Heavenly Father and us his children to be at one. Because of Jesus Christ—his life, his suffering, his death—we have been delivered from the powers of evil which beset us and prevent us from this at-one-ment. As Paul put it, "God was in Christ reconciling the world to himself" (2 Cor. 5:19).

See Forgiveness, Justification, Reconciliation, Redemption, Salvation, Sin.

Awe

AWE is the overwhelming feeling which comes over us in the presence of God. It is reverence in a high key, a combination of adoration and wonder and even fear. When we realize that he whom we worship created us, redeems us, (i.e., restores us to the status of God's faithful children), sustains us, and is the Eternal Judge, we are overwhelmed by his grandeur and majesty. We tremble in his presence; we are overcome by our awareness of his greatness. "The fear of the Lord" mentioned in Scriptures means not so much being scared as it means wonder and veneration. When the psalmist asks, "Who is like the Lord our God, who sits enthroned on high, but stoops to behold the heavens and the earth?" (Ps. 113:5), he is giving voice to his sense of awe.

See Fear of God.

B

Baptism

HOLY BAPTISM is the sacrament (i.e., a religious rite with deep spiritual meaning) through which a person is born into God's family, the Christian church, and given his or her Christian name.

Baptism in the early Church was an acting out of the death-and-resurrection motif and applying it to the candidate's own life. The person being baptized went down under the water—dead to the old sinful self and in a watery grave—then, coming up out of the water, became a new person in Christ, receiving the Spirit of the Risen Lord. This view of baptism comes straight out of the New Testament.

> Do you not know that all of us who have been baptized into Christ Jesus were baptized into his death? We were buried therefore with him by baptism into death, so that as Christ was raised from the dead by the glory of the Father, we too might walk in newness life. (Rom. 6:3–4; see also Col. 2:12)

This sacrament is a solemn agreement or covenant that the candidate (through sponsors, or godparents, if the candidate is an infant) makes with God. The way this covenant is set forth varies, but generally it follows this pattern: The candidate for baptism (or the sponsors) renounces allegiance to spiritual forces which draw us away from the love of God. He or she then accepts Jesus Christ as Lord and Savior, and in Episcopal and Lutheran Churches the ancient catechetical form of the Apostles' Creed is used to signify this. There may also be questions and promises regarding the candidate's future Christian living and learning.

God's part of this covenant is that the candidate is born anew by water and the Holy Spirit, sins are forgiven, and he or she becomes a member of Christ's Body, the Church. So the candidate becomes God's child by adoption and grace (Rom. 8:15; Eph 1:7, KJV).

Every family has a "spirit" of its own. In the divine family the spirit is God's Spirit, bestowed in baptism, which will sustain the person in a new life of grace and give him or her the courage to persevere. It is important, therefore, that the baptized person join with the other members of the family of God for prayer and praise, for forgiveness and guidance, and for the renewing strength found at the Lord's Table. Baptism is the time when awareness of the presence and operation of the Spirit in the life of the Church and in his or her own life is sharpened and confirmed.

Here are questions that need to be clarified with respect to baptism:

Are not all of us, baptized or not, God's children? All of us are God's creatures; he made us and we are precious to him. We are thus his children in the sense that the coffee table I made or the poem I wrote is "my brain child." But there is a world of difference between a brain-child relationship and that which I have with my baby daughter who holds my finger, smiles and says, "Da-Da." Coffee tables and poems do not and cannot respond. In baptism we receive his Spirit, become his adopted sons and daughters, and respond. "God has sent the Spirit of his Son into our hearts, crying, "Abba! [meaning] Father!" (Gal. 4:6). Jesus Christ is *the* Son of God; in baptism we become God's children by adoption and grace.

Why baptize infants who cannot understand what is happening? In early times, when adults were baptized their children were baptized along with them and brought up in the Christian faith (Acts 16:33). So the practice of baptizing infants is a venerable one. Those churches that baptize infants take this position. The Christian church is not an organization like a garden club or the Rotary, which a mature person decides to join when he or she understands the obligations of membership. Rather the Church is God's family. We are never too young to become members of a family. Parents and godparents or sponsors take the baptismal vows on behalf of the little ones in the family of God. In the Presbyterian church there are no godparents. The parents and the whole congregation are responsible for seeing that the infant is nurtured in the Christian faith. Then, when children are old enough to speak for themselves, they may renew those vows at confirmation, sometimes called the "commissioning of the baptized member."

See Anointing, Born-again, Church, Creed, Godparents, Holy Spirit, Name, Sacrament.

Bible

THE BIBLE is a collection of sacred books about God's dealings with the human race from the beginning of the world through the first century of the Christian era. The word *Bible* means "books." The Bible is divided into two parts—the Old Testament, covering the period from Creation to the beginning of the Christian era, and the New Testament covering the period from the birth of Jesus Christ through the first several generations of the Christian church.

There are about sixty-six books in the Old Testament. Both the number of these books and the order in which they stand varies depending upon which authority one accepts. There is no historical account of the formation of the Old Testament canon. (The canon of the Bible is that accepted list of books considered authentic and inspired.) The Christian church inherited the Scripture of the Old Testament from the Jewish people.

THE SEPTUAGINT is the Greek version of the Old Testament. Tradition says it was translated by seventy or seventy-two Jewish scholars at the request of Ptolemy II of Egypt. Most modern scholars believe that only the Pentateuch (the first five books) were completed in the early part of the third century B.C., and that the remaining books were translated in the next two centuries.

By the end of the second century A.D. there was a collection of apostolic documents later to be known as the New Testament, generally recognized as authoritative Scripture. From that time onward the idea of a body of authoritative Christian Scripture was a presupposition of all theologians. By the fourth century A.D. the list of books included in the new Testament canon was generally agreed upon.

THE VULGATE is the Latin version of the Bible which was prepared chiefly by Saint Jerome at the end of the fourth century and used as the authorized version in liturgical services throughout the Roman Catholic church. This was the practice until the Second Vatican Council initiated a change. The word *Vulgate* refers to the fact that Jerome's new translation was in the vulgar tongue, that is, in the common language spoken by the general public which in the fourth century was Latin. Now, Roman Catholic services are mostly conducted in the language commonly spoken by the local people.

In addition to the Old and New Testaments, there are the books of the Apocrypha discussed in this volume.

We call the Bible "the Word of God." The Bible is about people and what happens to them because God is at work in his world. So the Bible is first of all about God and what he is doing; God is the "hero." In it God is acting. He makes humankind in his own image and he loves his creation. But his human children take it upon themselves to run their own lives apart from him; they become sinners. The Bible is the story of God's consequent acts on our behalf—giving the Law, sending the prophets, then Jesus Christ who suffered and died for us, and finally the Holy Spirit in the life of the Christian church. We think of this story as the drama of Redemption, humanity's off-again-on-again relation with God.

That drama has its present application, for through it God is speaking to us as well as to those who have gone before us. When we read, "The Lord is my shepherd, I shall not want" (Ps. 23:1), we do not think of it primarily as a bit of poetry written around 1000 B.C. Rather, it speaks directly to us in the present: "The Lord is *my* shepherd, *I* shall not want." So the Bible, like no other book, has an eternal quality which we describe as the inspired Word of God.

To speak of the Bible as inspired means that the Holy Spirit inspired its various authors; *inspire* literally means "to breathe in." God's Spirit breathes into and works through individual writers to convey his truths and insights. In the same way, Handel was inspired to compose the "Hallelujah Chorus." Divine inspiration is sometimes thought to mean that because God's Spirit is inspiring the individual he cannot make any mistakes. If such were the case the individual would not be a person; he or she would be a machine in God's hands, like a typewriter or word processor. But God makes us persons, not puppets. Only in this way are we free to love him and be his children. It is the Spirit of this loving God who inspired the Bible's writers. Each is a person in his own right. Some are capable of great and generous insights like: "The Lord is full of compassion and mercy, slow to anger and of great kindness" (Ps. 103:8). Others have more narrow horizons and are less generous: "Rise up, O Lord; set me free, O my God; surely, you will strike all my enemies across the face, you will break the teeth of the wicked" (Ps. 3:7). It is fallible human beings whom God inspires and through whom he conveys his Eternal Word.

The Bible is the Church's book. It was the leaders of the Church under the guidance of the Holy Spirit who determined which books were to be considered Holy Scriptures—which would be "canonical," that is, accepted as inspired and authoritative. The Church, therefore, under the guidance of the Holy Spirit is the logical interpreter of what the Bible teaches. But at the same time individuals in their prayerful reading of the Bible find comfort and inspiration and guidance.

See Apocrypha, Canon, Covenant, Fundamentalism, Septuagint.

Blasphemy

BLASPHEMY is the act of reviling or of treating God irreverently. In the Old Testament times cursing the name of God was a crime punishable by death (Lev. 24:14–16). One of the Ten Commandments condemns taking the name of God "in vain." God's name is taken in vain when it is used vainly, lightly, or unthinkingly. Such an act is one of treating "the High and Lofty One that inhabits eternity" (Isa. 57:15) casually, disrespectfully, and blasphemously. How often in trivial talk people say, "O God this," "O God that," or say "O God it's hot." Such careless utterances are sheer blasphemy. They grate on the ears of serious believers.

See Name.

Blessing

THE BLESSING pronounced in worship, by a priest or other minister, often with upraised hand and the sign of the cross, is the way of saying that in God's Name those being blessed are declared to be holy. *Benediction* is the Anglicized form of the Latin word for blessing.

Whenever the word *bless* occurs in intercessions it is asking for a special gift or favor bestowed by God. This practice, especially in our private devotions, runs the danger of being meaningless, "Bless Jane and Billy and Myrtle and Sue . . ." can be rattled off unthinkingly. It can be a rigamarole of mumbo-jumbo one could recite in one's sleep. Cut your list down to a few people for whom you desire some particular gift or favor from the Father of us all. Then *bless* comes into its own as a venerable word which we use sparingly but with deep sincerity.

Blessing also refers to ourselves. We say, "I am blessed with good health," or "I am blessed with loyal friends."

"Count your Blessings" is a popular hymn in some churches. One's evening devotions could follow that pattern with profit. Probably some such practice caused the psalmist to write, "Turn again to your rest, O my soul, for the Lord has treated you well" (Ps. 116:6). The Almighty and Merciful Lord has bestowed blessings on each of us, many of which we take for granted. It is easy to fail to appreciate evidences of God's loving kindness. But such insensitivity is in part responsible when one's spiritual life becomes thin.

When blessing refers to some object it is a heavenward request for special favor to those who will be making use of it. For instance, during the marriage service in some churches, the officiant says, "Bless, O Lord, this ring."

When the word bless is directed to God it is an expression of praise and devotion and worship. "Bless the Lord, O my soul, and all that is within me, bless his holy Name" (Ps. 103:1).

Born-Again

BORN-AGAIN CHRISTIANS are those who at a moment of conversion have turned to the Lord and accepted him as their Savior. Their way of life has definitely changed as a result of that occurrence. The experience of Saul (later to become Paul) on the Damascus Road (Acts 9:1–22) is this type of religious happening. So is the experience of John Wesley in the Aldersgate Street Church, London, in 1738.

When born-again Christians speak of having been converted, a part of what they mean is that their lives have been turned around. Nicodemus in his encounter with Jesus discovered this possibility for the first time (John 3:1–8).

Actually, every Christian is a reborn person. He is first born into his human family. Then at holy baptism he is born again into God's family, the Christian Church. So by virtue of his baptism every Christian is a reborn believer. However, the term "born-again Christian" is used primarily to describe those who have had a conversion experience.

See Baptism.

C

Canon

CANON is a word of widely diverse meanings. Basically, it refers to a rule or a measure. Here are five uses of the word in religious circles:

1. The Bible: The *canon* of Holy Scriptures is the list of the books of the Bible that has been certified by the Church, and by Israel before her, as dependable channels of the Word of God. Christian churches are not in full agreement as to all of the books which constitute the canon of the Bible.
2. Liturgy: The *Canon* is a traditional term for the Great Thanksgiving in the Eucharist. Roman Catholics speak of the "Canon of the Mass." This is also referred to as the Prayer of Consecration or the "Great Thanksgiving."
3. Church law: *Canon* law is ecclesiastical law which has been enacted by a church council or other competent authority. The term may also be used to refer to the whole body of ecclesiastical law.
4. Hymnology: A musical *canon* is a tune which one group starts to sing, then (usually) on the eighth beat a second group starts at the beginning and the two groups sing together in harmony. The hymn "All Praise to Thee, My God, This Night" is set to a canon by the English composer Thomas Tallis. The familiar round, "Row, Row, Row Your Boat," follows the same pattern.
5. Title: A *canon* is a church official. Frequently the individual is a priest on the staff of a cathedral under the dean or provost. Sometimes the title is bestowed as a symbol of recognition— an honorary canon.

See Bible.

Catholic

CATHOLIC is the inclusive term which refers to the Church that claims unbroken lineage from New Testament times to the present and is custodian of the whole of Christian truth for all people in every age and in every place. Catholic means universal in the fullest possible sense.

The word is used to refer to members of the Roman Catholic church whose earthly head is the pope, the bishop of Rome. The other Catholic churches of Christendom include the Eastern Orthodox churches, and the Anglican churches (Church of England, the Episcopal church, and the other Anglican churches). All of them trace their lineage back to the Church of the New Testament, in contrast to those churches whose founders (such as Martin Luther and John Calvin) led their followers not only to break away from allegiance to the bishop of Rome, but also not to preserve continuity with the church's historic life back through the ages to the apostles.

At the time of the Reformation, the Church of England differed significantly from the Protestant churches on the Continent. The Anglicans, as they came to be known, also broke away from allegiance to the bishop of Rome, but they cherished their visible linkage with the past through the historic episcopacy. They carefully maintained apostolic succession connecting their bishops to the long line of their predecessors throughout the ages.

Even though Lutherans, Methodists, Presbyterians, and other Protestants do not consider apostolic succession important, they do believe in the Church universal whose truth has come down to us from New Testament times. And they seek to proclaim all of the truth our Lord taught.

See Apostolic Succession, Protestant.

Charismatic Christian

A CHARISMATIC CHRISTIAN is one who lays great stress on the fact that he or she has been "baptized with the Holy Spirit." This spiritual experience is evidenced by speaking with tongues (known as glossolalia).

In the New Testament, "baptized with the Holy Spirit" referred to the initial receiving of the Holy Spirit by the early believers in the Risen Lord. Peter recalls that while he was explaining his Resurrection belief to Cornelius, the Roman centurion, and his family, "the

Holy Spirit fell on them just as on us at the beginning [the apostles on the Day of Pentecost, Acts 2:1–4]. And I remembered the word of the Lord how he said, 'John baptized with water, but you shall be baptized with the Holy Spirit'" (Acts 11:15–16). This figure of speech – "baptized with the Holy Spirit"– is found only in the Book of Acts.

After World War I, there developed in America a yearning for expressions of religion which emphasized experience and feeling to a greater degree. So it was then that the biblical experience of being baptized with the Spirit began to take on deep significance.

Because Christians were first baptized with the Holy Spirit on the Day of Pentecost, Christians emphasizing this baptism came to be known as Pentecostals. In time this experience found its way into the life of mainline churches.

Not only do Charismatics speak with tongues – the language of angels (1 Cor.13:1) – they make a practice of laying hands on the person prayed for so that he or she may receive the Spirit. They engage in prophecy, and in healings – the sign of the new age. There is a lot of emotion, many expressions of "Praise the Lord," and hands lifted heavenward in song.

A part of the attraction of their meetings is that people find healing, ecstasy, and new status in their gatherings.

See Glossolalia.

Christ

CHRIST is a title meaning "the anointed one." The word christ comes from the Greek word christos; its Hebrew counterpart means "messiah." The title, "the anointed one," tells who a person is, what his role is. Kings in ancient times were anointed instead of being crowned; sacred oil was poured over them as a sign that they were set apart and dedicated to the role of governing their people (1 Sam. 9:27–10:1; 16:12–13). The coronation psalms of the Old Testament also illustrate this practice (e.g., Ps. 89:19–20). Basically, a messiah or christ was someone who had been consecrated or set apart for a particular work in the service of God.

The Old Testament looks forward to the coming of God's messiah who would save his people. The ideas of what he would be like varied. Some thought he would be like Moses, who led God's people out of slavery and gave them the Commandments. This second Moses would lead people into keeping the Law in some new and vital way—a great moral leader. Others thought the messiah would be a descendant of David, the warrior-king. This son of David would restore the ancient Hebrew kingdom and rebuild a worldwide Jewish empire. He would be the liberator of his people, freeing them from their oppressors. And a third view was that the messiah would be the Son of man described in Daniel's vision (Dan. 7:9–14, especially 7:13–14). He would be a supernatural being to whom, following God's judgment of the nations, the Lord of all would give everlasting dominion over all the peoples and nations of the earth.

The prophet Malachi said that Elijah would return before "the great and terrible day of the Lord" (Mal. 4:5)—that is, the coming of the messiah. So the preaching of John the Baptist (Luke 3:7–17) created a fever of expectation that the messiah would come at any moment. The popular hope was that the messiah would be a political champion, a warrior-king who would deliver God's people from their Roman oppressors.

Many people saw Jesus as possibly being the promised messiah, but he rejected the role of a political or military leader. When Peter finally put the Lord's identity into words, Jesus immediately explained what the term meant to him—suffering, death, and beyond it, resurrection (Luke 9:20–22). He thought of his messianic role as a blending of three Old Testament conceptions—the Son of David, the Son of man, and the Suffering Servant of the Lord. He was the Davidic king who would restore God's reign of justice and peace. He was also the Son of man, that heavenly figure who would bring both God's judgment and the rewarding of the persecuted saints of the Most High. And finally, he was the Servant of the Lord described in the Book of Isaiah (Isa. 52:13–53:12). His vicarious suffering and death would bring the nations to the knowledge of God. In Jesus' blending of these three roles primary importance was given to the establishment of God's kingdom and the realization of Israel's destiny as the holy people of God.

So Jesus is the Christ. Because of the kind of Christ he is, we can appreciate the centrality of the Kingdom of God in his teaching. We can also understand why words and phrases of the Lord's Prayer echo Daniel's vision, and why Isaiah's Suffering Servant poem is quoted throughout the account of the Lord's Passion.

See Anointing.

The Church

THE CHURCH is primarily the people of God, the community of those who have made the New Covenant with him when they were baptized. In normal parlance the word "church" means both the place where Christian believers meet – God's house – and the company of believers themselves. The Greek word, *ecclesia*, from which we get *ecclesiastic*, literally means "the called out assembly of people" (as by a town crier) who gather in the Lord's Name.

The community of believers is a vast throng on this side of the grave and beyond. We catch a glimpse of this multitude when in the "Te Deum" (a widely used, ancient hymn of praise) we sing:

> The glorious company of the Apostles praise thee.
> The goodly fellowship of the Prophets praise thee.
> The noble army of Martyrs praise thee.
> The holy Church throughout all the world doth acknowledge thee.

In the New Testament two figures of speech are principally used to describe the nature of the Church. One is "the Body of Christ." Christ is the head and each member of the Church is a member or part of the body – each different, but each necessary for the health of the whole body. "You are the body of Christ and individually members of it" (1 Cor. 12:27). Paul spells out this analogy in 1 Corinthians 12:14–31.

The Body of Christ description of the Church is a pleasing and reassuring one. It is very easy to assume that the Christian church is chiefly composed of the dignitaries up front on Sunday and those who make decisions and pronouncements at important meetings: *They* are the part of the Church that is important. I am just a back pew member whose "amens" are not even heard by the person in the next row.

This is not so.

Everybody counts and is important in the household of God, the Christian church. The Body of Christ is a delightfully appropriate description. For the well-being and contribution of every part is necessary in order that the physical body is healthy; when I have a toothache I ache all over. In the eyes of God all of his children are precious. In the eyes of God every member of the Church counts and is important. That is what the Body of Christ analogy says to us.

The Church is also described as the "Bride of Christ." This has Old Testament roots: "As the bridegroom rejoices over the bride, shall your God rejoice over you" (Isa. 62:1-5). The prophet thinks of the faithful of Israel as the Lord's bride. This analogy is only used to describe the relation of Christ to the Church in the last book of the Bible, "Then came one of the seven angels . . . to me, saying, 'Come, I will show you the Bride, the wife of the Lamb'" (Rev. 21:9); although it is implied in Ephesians 5:23-33.

Probably the most inclusive New Testament description of the Church is found in the First Letter of Peter:

> You are a chosen race, a royal priesthood, a holy nation, God's own people, that you may declare the wonderful deeds of him who called you out of darkness into his marvelous light. Once you were no people but now you are God's people, once you had not received mercy but now you have received mercy. (1 Pet. 2:9-10)

In the creeds the Church is described as one, holy, catholic, and apostolic. Here is what these words mean:

> The Church is *one*, because it is one Body, under one Head, our Lord Jesus Christ.
> The Church is *holy*, because the Holy Spirit dwells in it, consecrates its members, and guides them to do God's work.
> The Church is *catholic*, because it proclaims the whole faith to all people, to the end of time.
> The Church is *apostolic*, because it continues in the teaching and fellowship of the apostles and is sent to carry out Christ's mission to all people. (Book of Common Prayer, p. 854)

See Baptism, Catholic, Holy Spirit.

Church Year

THE CHURCH YEAR is the calendar pattern of Christian observance of the great biblical events upon which our faith is based. Think of it as the Bible tacked down on the calendar.

There are seven seasons of the Church year.

ADVENT, the four Sundays before Christmas Day, tells us of the preparation for the coming of our Lord as the Babe of Bethlehem, and bids us prepare for his Second Coming to judge the world. It is a time of anticipation, a time of penitence and resolve so that we shall be ready to greet the Lord when he comes. *Advent* means "coming."

CHRISTMAS commemorates the Nativity of our Lord—the coming of God's Son into the world. Early Christians did not lay as great a stress on Jesus' birthday as on the fact that God's Son died for us and rose again. Thus they celebrated Easter as commemorating the Resurrection, but it was nearly three hundred years before the Western church (centering at Rome) set December 25 as the day for the Nativity observance. The Eastern church (centering at Constantinople) holds a similar observance on January 6. In the West we observe both of these celebrations, making December 25 the time to give thanks for the Lord's incarnation (his coming in the flesh) and January 6 the time to celebrate the wonderful ways he is revealed to be God's Son and Savior of the world. Christmastide is the name for the Christmas season which runs through January 6—the twelve days of Christmas of the familiar carol.

EPIPHANY is a wider-stage celebration of the Christmas fact. We hear the accounts of the ways in which Jesus is revealed to be God's Son. The Greek word *epiphany* means "to make manifest" or "to shine forth." We celebrate the meaning and implication for the world of Christ's coming. Here is outreach, buoyancy, challenge. The awed contemplation of Christmas has now been replaced by action.

> Spread the glory of redemption
> 'Til all the world thy saving grace shall know. (Hymn, "Awake Thou Spirit of the Watchman")

LENT is a forty-day season of preparation for Easter. The first day of Lent has been called "Ash Wednesday" since the ninth century because of the practice of marking the brows of the faithful with ashes, a symbol both of the recipients' penitence and mortality, and of the penitential nature of the Lenten season. In the early Church,

Lent was the period of preparation of candidates for baptism. The all-night vigil at the end of Lent on the eve of Easter came to a climax with the baptism of those persons. Then the newly baptized members of the Church joined with their Christian sisters and brothers in the celebration of the first Easter Eucharist. The season of Lent begins with our remembrance of the Lord's forty days of spiritual preparation in the wilderness after his baptism and before he began his ministry. So it is a time of spiritual discipline and of self-denial. G.K. Chesterton once said, "A white post will only continue to be a white post if it is painted white every year; otherwise it will become a black post." Our lives are like that. We Christians need to have an annual retraining period. Otherwise our souls become tarnished, our prayers mere words, our service selfish, and our giving trivial. Lent is a time of renewal, of retraining, of relearning.

HOLY WEEK is the last week of Lent and commemorates the events of the last week of Jesus' earthly life. Palm Sunday was the day of his triumphal ride into Jerusalem. Maundy Thursday celebrates the institution of the Lord's Supper. It takes its name from the Latin reading of Jesus' words on that occasion: "A new commandment [*mandatum*] I give to you, that you love one another; even as I have loved you" (John 13:34). Good Friday is the "Day of the Cross." It was in England that the name "Good Friday" came into general use. The emphasis is thus put on the blessings which are ours because "God shows his love for us in that while we were yet sinners Christ died for us" (Rom. 5:8).

The Crucifixion-Resurrection took place at the time of the Jewish Feast of the Passover. The word *paschal*, from the Greek word for Passover, is used by Christians to refer to that which is Easter-related. The Paschal Vigil is the Easter Vigil. The Paschal Candle burns during the fifty days of Eastertide as a sign of the Resurrection.

EASTER celebrates the Lord's Resurrection from the dead. This earliest of Christian seasons covers forty days ending with Ascension Day. During that time in the early Church neither fasting nor kneeling were permitted. It was a time of joy, excitement, and sheer wonder that God had raised Jesus Christ from the dead. Members of the early Church prepared to celebrate this great feast first with an all-night vigil, later with forty hours, then a week, then several weeks, and finally, after four hundred years, with the full-blown season of Lent as we know it. For them the preparation and the celebration went together. The Lord's death and Resurrection were of a piece—a single event in two parts—and one could not be understood without the other. Only as we pay serious attention to our Lord's Passion and death will Easter dawn upon us as a new day in which to rejoice and be glad.

ASCENSION celebrates the Risen Lord's triumphal return to heaven (Acts 1:1-11). Notice that the Ascension hymns have a majestic tone and a coronation flavor. It is because "God has highly exalted him and bestowed on him the name which is above every name. . . . Jesus Christ is the Lord, to the glory of God the Father" (Phil. 2:9-11).

PENTECOST commemorates the coming of the Holy Spirit. The event took place on the Jewish feast day which occurred fifty days after the Passover (Acts 2:1-11). *Pentecost* means "fiftieth." The Feast of the Fiftieth Day has several Old Testament names: the Feast of the Harvest (Exod. 23:14), the Feast of Weeks (Deut. 16:10), the Day of the Firstfruits (Num. 28:26). But regardless of its name, it was one of the three great agricultural festivals on which all males were required to make a pilgrimage to the Temple at Jerusalem (Exod. 34:18, 22-23; 2 Chron. 8:12-13). It was on this great festival in the Jewish calendar that the Spirit of God who once spoke through the prophets, then was embodied in Jesus, now became the Spirit of the Church—the inspiration and guide of its members individually and corporately. On this day the Church started to grow. It was possessed of a new life full of love and joy, of power and hope. All shared the Spirit and were bound together by the Spirit's influence. The experience was so full of meaning for those who believed in the Crucified and Risen Lord that the Jewish feast of Pentecost became a great Christian festival equal to Easter and Christmas. The awed awareness of Good Friday and Easter had now been replaced by an audacious reaching out in order to bring all people to a knowledge of God's saving power and love. Read Acts 2; it is the story of the first Christian Pentecost and of the immediate effect on the believers.

The feast of Pentecost came to be called "Whitsunday" in England. A logical reason (although it may not be historical) is that the term *Whitsunday* is a contraction of *White Sunday*. Because of the climate in England, the eve of Pentecost, rather than the eve of Easter became the time for baptisms (by immersion) because the weather is warmer then. The day was nicknamed for the white robes worn by the candidates for baptism.

There are some other occasions which are regularly observed by various branches of Christendom which do not fit into the Bible-oriented pattern of the Church year. There are saints days on which the apostles and other New Testament persons are remembered. The Roman Catholics and Episcopalians considerably enlarge this list to include a number of saints of the ages who have been "the lights of the world in their several generations" (*Book of Common Prayer*, p. 487). All Saints' Day, November 1, is the day Roman Catholics, Lutherans, Episcopalians, Methodists, and perhaps others remember their own special "saints." All Saints' Day is the chief of saints' days because it is both all-inclusive and very personal.

Halloween is a by-product of All Saints' Day observance. The word *Halloween* is a contraction of *All Hallows' Eve*, the eve of All Saints' Day. The legend was that on the eve of the commemoration of good and noble souls, evil and mischievous spirits roamed abroad and had a final fling before the day of the more worthy spirits dawned.

See Holy Spirit, Sunday, Vigil.

Circumcision

CIRCUMCISION is the Jewish name-giving ceremony for male children. Cutting, scarring, or tattooing some part of the body as a sign of "belonging" is an ancient custom among certain peoples. The word *circumcision* comes from the Latin word for "cutting around."

Among the Jews, circumcision was the rite in which a small portion of loose skin was cut from the penis of a male baby. It came to be thought of as a religious requirement, a seal of the covenant God had made with Abraham (Gen. 17:19–27). Since the baby Jesus was a Jewish boy, he was circumcised and received his name on his eighth day (Luke 2:21). The Christian Feast of the Holy Name on January 1 celebrates this occasion.

Christian baptism has a purpose somewhat like circumcision. It is the seal of the new covenant in Christ. In it the child receives his or her name as an individual in God's family.

See Baptism.

Collect

A COLLECT (pronounced *COL-lect*) is a specific form of written prayer which has been a part of our Christian liturgical heritage since about the fifth century. The name derives from the Gallican (Roman) rite (*collectio*, later *collecto*) and refers to the function of the prayer, to its collecting or summing up of the peoples' intercessions.

Just as we can divide poetry into different types of poems such as the ballad, the sonnet, and the lyric, so we can distinguish between different types of prayer. One of these is the collect.

A collect is generally direct, well-balanced, and uses an economy of words. Almost all collects are short, only a single sentence. But not every short prayer is a collect, for the main thing that makes a prayer a collect is its pattern. Of these patterns, two are very easy to recognize.

The first type of collect has a five-part pattern: *(1)* the prayer opens by calling upon God; *(2)* a "who" clause follows, mentioning something we believe about God which is the reason why this prayer is addressed to him; *(3)* then comes the asking clause; followed by *(4)* the hoped-for result; and *(5)* the conclusion. Here is a collect from *The Book of Common Prayer* built on this pattern. The italicized numbers show each of the five parts included in the pattern:

Almighty God	*(1)*
unto whom all hearts are open,	*(2)*
all desires known,	
and from whom no secrets are hid;	
Cleanse the thoughts of our hearts	*(3)*
by the inspiration of thy Holy Spirit,	
that we may perfectly love thee,	*(4)*
and worthily magnify thy holy Name;	
through Christ our Lord.	*(5)*

The second type of collect begins with an imperative verb such as "give" or "send." The clause that starts off with this verb is the asking clause, in which we ask God for something that we feel we need very much (1). After that the collect goes on to say what we think will be the happy result if God actually gives us the thing we ask of him (2). Finally, there is the ending, usually something like "through Jesus Christ our Lord," which means, "we ask this in the Spirit of Jesus" (3). Here is a familiar evening collect from *The Book of Common Prayer* built on this pattern:

Lighten our darkness, we beseech thee, O Lord;	(1)
and by thy great mercy defend us from all perils	(2)
and dangers of this night,	
for the love of thy only Son, our Savior Jesus Christ.	(3)

If you read this out loud, you will notice that it is almost poetry. The finest collects have rhythm and balance something like poetry.

In many branches of Christendom there is a special collect for every Sunday and Holy Day.

Commandments

God's COMMANDMENTS are his laws addressed to us. The Ten Commandments are those that he gave Moses on Mount Sinai (Exod. 19:1–20:20). (*Decalogue* is Greek for Ten Commandments.) These represent the basic content of the Law of God and have eternal value.

Down through the centuries, following the days of the children of Israel in the wilderness, their religious teachers—priests and rabbis—explained and elaborated on the meaning of each particular commandment. In time these refinements became codified and fixed; they came to be thought of as having the weight and authority of the original ten. By the time of Jesus the Ten Commandments had thus been amplified into over seven hundred laws.

For example, one Commandment states, "Remember the Sabbath day, to keep it holy. Six days you shall labor, and do all your work; but the seventh is the Sabbath of the Lord your God; in it you shall not do any work" (Exod. 20:8–10). What constitutes "work"? Washing clothes, certainly. But what about washing dishes or bathing? How far can you walk on the Sabbath without working? "A Sabbath Day's journey" was a legally determined distance (see Acts 1:12). So it was that that Commandment had been stretched out into thirty-six regulations.

The Law (and it is always used in the singular in the New Testament) was considered the holy will of God. But in Jesus' day the Law was thought to include all its seven hundred-odd elaborations. No one except full-time religious teachers like the Pharisees, could know, let alone keep, all of it. So the Law became a barrier between people and God. Jesus' running battle with the Pharisees was on this subject. Jesus repeatedly attacked the system (Mark 2:27; 3:1-6; John 9:13-16). He helped ordinary people find their way back into God's presence.

In order to appreciate the full authority of the Ten Commandments, notice that they are never called the "Ten Laws of God." Laws are impersonal, neutral, impartial. They have a sort of independent existence; they are external. We are tempted to try to beat the law and not get caught. For example, we drive over the speed limit while watching the rearview mirror lest a policeman catch us. Commandments are different. Commandments are personal—they are addressed to each individual directly by his superior. God's Commandments are the Heavenly Father's will and he addresses each of us his human children. The Ten Commandments do not say it is unlawful to kill or steal or bear false witness against another. Rather, they say: "YOU shall not kill." "YOU shall not steal." "YOU shall not bear false witness against YOUR neighbor." There is a big difference. Jesus talked about "the will of my Father in Heaven."

Communion of Saints

COMMUNION OF SAINTS means the dependence of all of us in the Church on each other. This analogy suggests something of the intended meaning of the term "Communion of Saints": if you planned to climb a high mountain, up precipices and over snow and ice, you would go with a party, and the guide would rope the group together so if you slipped the others could hold you or pull you back to safety.

Christians need each other. On the long climb to heaven there are many slippery places. We'd be fools to climb alone. We let our Lord "rope" us together in the fellowship of his Church by baptism. We draw the rope of fellowship tighter when we take part in the Holy Eucharist (or Mass or Holy Communion). If we slip and fall, we let our line of fellow climbers pull us back by absolution (i.e., forgiveness and acceptance).

Who gives the strongest pull? Why, of course, those who have climbed on ahead—in other words, the saints in heaven. Whether we ask them or not, whether we even think of them or not, they are "pulling for us" all the time. So it is that our dependence on each other has come to be called the "Communion of Saints."

You may not have realized it but you are a "saint." In the New Testament all baptized Christians are called "saints." The Greek word actually means "the holy ones." We are "holy" because we belong to the company of God's people whose esprit de corps is the Holy Spirit. That company, of course, includes those who have climbed ahead. William How described the Communion of Saints this way in his hymn "For all the Saints":

> O blest communion, fellowship divine!
> We feebly struggle, they in glory shine;
> Yet all are one in thee, for all are thine. Alleluia!

See Absolution, Church, Holy Spirit.

Confession

CONFESSION is owning up to guilt. A prayer of confession is one in which we tell God we are sorry for the wrong we have done. Basically, confession is the humble courage which enables one to say, "I was wrong; I am sorry."

If as a child you disobeyed your parents, suffered in your separation from them in spirit if not in body, then said, "I am sorry," and were welcomed back into the bosom of your family, you know that this "confession" is what your parents wanted. With it separation stopped and reconciliation began. Probably they did all they could to help you, for they wanted you back as a member of the family in good standing. So it is with God. He does all in his power to help us wake up to our need and come back to him. The Parable of the Prodigal Son (Luke 15:11–32) is all downhill until the wandering prodigal comes to himself, recognizes that his own willfulness and selfishness have brought him to his present state and separated him from a happy relationship with his father. He resolves to go to him and confess; then something wonderful happens. His father sees him coming, runs to meet him, interrupts his rehearsed words of confession with exciting plans for celebrating his restoration to his place in the family.

Our selfishness and willfulness shut us out from our rightful relationship to God as his faithful children. Sometimes in the privacy of our own prayers we are able to tell God how truly sorry we are and ask his forgiveness. But sometimes this is not enough. We need to say out loud that we are sorry and to hear with our ears that God forgives us. This may be a private confession in the presence of a priest or pastor. Upon hearing the words of absolution and the dismissal, "Go in peace, for the Lord has put away your sin," your sense of guilt is removed and you experience the joy of being forgiven.

Others experience this same forgiveness through taking part in a general confession in a church service and accepting as one's very own the words of the priest or minister, "Almighty . . . God pardon and deliver you (us) from all your (our) sins, confirm and strengthen you (us) in all goodness and bring you (us) to everlasting life" (*Book of Common Prayer*, p. 332). To which you reply with all your heart, "AMEN."

Theodore Wedel spoke of the Church as the company of penitent and forgiven sinners. Confession establishes our place in that company.

See Absolution, Forgiveness, Holy Spirit, Penitence, Sin.

Confirmation

CONFIRMATION is the rite of commissioning a member of the Church. One who has been baptized with water in the Name of the Holy Trinity is a full-fledged Christian. However, in churches where infants are baptized, there is a subsequent rite called confirmation

in which after due preparation, they "make a mature public affirmation of their faith and commitment to the responsibilities of their
baptism" (*Book of Common Prayer*, p. 412).

Confirmation is the rite in which one publicly assumes one's
role as a responsible Christian. The word *confirm* is used in two
ways. First it means to ratify or to renew; in confirmation the candidate renews the promises made on his or her behalf at baptism. The
second meaning is to fill with steadfastness, determination,
strength. It emphasizes the strengthening power of the Holy Spirit
which enables the Christian to carry out his or her intended ministry in the world. This is dramatically demonstrated when the bishop,
or in some churches the minister lays hands on the confirmand's
head and prays, that he or she be strengthened for service by the
Holy Spirit. Regardless of denomination, the confirmands confirm
or renew their baptismal vows; God confirms or strengthens the
individual with his Holy Spirit.

Since the fifth century, the Church has marked the occasion
when a mature person accepted responsibility for service to Christ
and his Kingdom. The Reformation churches wrought changes in
the form but not in the intent of the confirmation rite. In every case,
the individual is sent forth strengthened and renewed by the Holy
Spirit to bear witness to God's love and saving power.

See Baptism, Ministry.

Consecration

CONSECRATION means to set apart for or dedicate to God's holy purposes. At the Holy Eucharist, the Great Thanksgiving (also called,
the Canon of the Mass or the Prayer of Consecration) is that part of
the liturgy during which the celebrant prays that the bread and
wine may be sanctified by God's Holy Spirit to be our spiritual food.
Churches differ as to their interpretation of what exactly is meant
when the bread and wine are consecrated and become for the faithful the Body and Blood of Christ. For some the eucharistic miracle
takes place: the bread and wine have in truth become the Body and
Blood of Jesus sacrificed for us. Others disclaim any miracle saying
only that the service is a memorial remembrance of the Last Supper.
And there are various shades of interpretation in 'between. But

regardless of differences, all agree that in that holy meal, instituted by our Lord, God's faithful people are spiritually fed and strengthened for his service.

See Eucharist, Transubstantiation.

Covenant

A COVENANT is a solemn agreement. In legal terms we would call it a contract. The Bible is the story of the solemn agreement or covenant between God and his people. The Old Testament (the word *testament* means "covenant") is about the Old Covenant between God and Israel; the New Testament is about the New Covenant established through Christ with the New Israel, the Christian Church.

Under the Old Covenant between God and Abraham, Abraham was to be faithful to God and God would make Abraham "father of a multitude of nations." This was sealed with blood (Gen. 17:1-11). God renewed this covenant at Mount Sinai with Moses, representing the children of Israel. "I shall be your God and you shall be my people" (Lev. 26:12). Obey my commandments and you shall be my people, God promised; the story is told in Exodus 19-20.

The New Covenant or Testament is between God in Christ and those faithful to him. The scene is the Last Supper. Jesus sums up the meaning of his approaching death when he raises his cup of wine and says, "This cup which is poured out is the New Covenant in my blood" (Luke 22:20). The covenant is sealed with the blood of Jesus.

The New Covenant in Jesus Christ goes beyond that of Moses' day which said, "If you obey God, he will love you." The New Covenant says that when we do not obey him we in a sense crucify the Lord afresh. We cause him to suffer the consequences of our sin. He still loves us and prays for our forgiveness. He does not break covenant with us. We see this willing, suffering, divine love in the Passion and death of Jesus Christ. That is why the Cross is the central symbol of New Testament faith.

After the Lord's Resurrection, he bestowed the Holy Spirit on the company of believers, now the Christian Church. Converts became members of that company through being baptized, that is, through entering into the Baptismal Covenant. In that rite, as we perform it today, God bestows his forgiveness and the candidates become his children by adoption and grace (Rom. 8:15; Eph. 1:7, KJV). The covenant is sealed by the Holy Spirit, usually with the sign of the cross on the candidates' foreheads.

The Lord's Supper is the covenant meal of those who have shared in the Baptismal Covenant. For at that Table we receive "the holy food of new and unending life in him" (*Book of Common Prayer*, p. 363), a profound renewing of our covenant with him.

See Baptism, Bible.

Covet

TO COVET is to desire wrongfully what belongs to someone else. It is not wrong to want things. But it is very wrong to want something that belongs to someone else so keenly that you will scheme to get it or will hurt the person who has it. It is normal to want things and to be ambitious for honors. But when this natural urge injures a relationship with others it becomes covetousness. And covetousness is like a trap door; once it is opened one finds oneself on murky steps leading down into other sins against one's neighbor.

The Bible story of Naboth's vineyard illustrates this in the extreme (1 Kings 21:1–20). Ahab, king of Samaria, wants the vineyard of his neighbor Naboth. But Naboth refuses to sell his precious, ancestral property to the king. Ahab broods over this and covets the vineyard. Then Queen Jezebel comes to his assistance. She is the daughter of the king of Tyre and has brought to Samaria the gods of her homeland. She cares nothing for the commandments of God. She does in fact secure Naboth's vineyard for King Ahab, but in the process she breaks not only the commandment, "Thou shalt not covet," but at least three others—those prohibiting false witness, murder, and stealing. Read the whole story in 1 Kings 21; the voice of the prophet Elijah at the end is, for Ahab, the voice of God condemning him.

We can see why one of the commandments is, "Thou shalt not covet." As soon as we begin to covet that which belongs to someone else the friendly feeling of camaraderie and of belonging together disappears. This is true everywhere—at home, in athletics, at school, in business. And wars have resulted when a nation has coveted the raw materials or natural resources or territory belonging to another nation.

See Commandments, Sin.

Creation

CREATION is God's act of making everything—the universe, the world and all its inhabitants. To say that God is the Creator of all things means that behind the whole process of being made or born, God's creative love is at work.

We know something about what creation is like because we make things ourselves. When we go to the workbench or sewing machine or typewriter or canvas, we give expression to an idea we have. We have a purpose in mind, whether it is to make a birdhouse, a dress, a story, or a picture. What we turn out may not be perfect, but it is ours, our creation.

However, what we make has to be shaped out of something else God has made. But God created everything out of *nothing*! The Bible tells us this. It does not tell us *how* he did it. The "how" is the province of science. No one would turn to poetry in seeking mechanical knowledge. And no one should expect to find scientific explanations in Holy Scriptures, the account of God's mighty acts of creation and redemption. The proper attitude toward the two Genesis stories of creation—Genesis 1:1–2:4 and 2:4–25—is that of reverence, awe, and praise. Christopher Smart's hymn, "We sing of God the Mighty Source" illustrates it:

> We sing of God, the mighty source
> Of all things; the stupendous force
> On which all strength depends;
> From whose right arm, beneath whose eyes,
> All period, power, and enterprise
> Commences, reigns, and ends. (The Hymnal 1982 (1985), p. 386)

The scientist looks into a telescope, a microscope, and at the findings of archaeological "digs" seeking to learn something of *how* God did it.

The Bible never attempts to answer the question "how?" *That* God did it is the important biblical consideration, and that conviction is stated several times, not just in the two creation stories in Genesis. The Book of Job prefers to speak of creation as a dawning (not "six days")—when "the morning stars sang together and all the sons of God shouted for joy" (Job 38:7). It is arbitrary to contend that Job is poetic and Genesis is literal. The point is that they are different. The writer of Proverbs offers yet another perspective on cosmic origins. There "Wisdom" is made to speak and says of herself that she was created by God before anything else and then became the instrument by which all other things were fashioned (Prov. 8:22–31). Still again, the poetry of Isaiah speaks of creation as something occurring "now, not long ago"; that is, occurring in the historic upheavals of our own time (Isa. 48:7). So it is that the Bible says in several ways that God is the Creator and it leaves the mechanics of how he did it to the scientists.

People are a wonderful part of God's creation. He did not make us like puppets on a string, but rather as persons who can respond to him, love him, and praise him. But even God cannot buy love; we have to be free to love him. The freedom God gives us means that, like Adam and Eve, we can rebel against him and seek to be God's rivals instead of his children (Gen. 3:1–24). And, like Cain, we can have murderous feelings (Gen. 4:1–10); we can hurt each other in all sorts of ways.

On the other hand, a part of God's purpose is that we will love him as he loves us. That is why the Bible is the story of redemption (i.e., of making good and acceptable again) as well as of creation; God wants his rebellious children to return to him. That is why "God so loved the world that he sent his Son."

Creation is an ongoing process; God continues to be the Creator and to keep his universe in existence for the world is incomplete and keeps developing according to his purpose.

See Predestination, Redemption.

Creed

A CREED is an official statement of belief. For the Christian the faith of the Church is summed up in the Apostles' and Nicene Creeds.

The roots of the Apostles' Creed go back to the second century A.D., hence its name. This is the way it probably came into being. In the account of the imprisonment of Paul and Silas in Philippi, because of their preaching and healing (Acts 16:16–34), the climax comes following an earthquake when the shaken jailor asks Paul, "What must I do to be saved?" The apostle replies, "Believe on the name of the Lord Jesus." That statement phrased as a question addressed to the candidate for baptism is probably the beginning of the baptismal credal statement which developed during the next five generations into what we now know as the Apostles' Creed. The interrogatory form of this creed found in the Episcopal rite of holy baptism and the Lutheran rite of confirmation is probably its very ancient form. That creed has the authority of church practice from very early times.

The Nicene Creed is of a different origin. It is the official statement of the first General Council of the Christian Church in A.D. 325 and emphasizes the divinity of our Lord and the work of the Holy Spirit. Because it was drawn up by a body of people, its original form was in the plural: "We believe in God. . . ." The Nicene Creed comes to us with the authority of the responsible leaders of the ancient Church—bishops and theologians.

Both creeds have the authority of the Church behind them. Both state our belief about what God has done and is doing. Our belief hinges on the little word "in": when we say "I believe *in* God . . ." a personal relationship is implied. If the creed were an argument it would state, "I believe *that* there is a God who . . ." There is a world of difference between those two statements. Substitute the name of your next door neighbor and you will see how great a difference there is between "believing in" and "believing that." When I believe *in* my neighbor we are trusting friends, and that is what the creed is saying. "I believe *in* God" means that I am personally involved with him. He cares about me and sent his Son into the world "for us and for our salvation." I love him. I trust him. I want to serve him faithfully. When we say "I believe" or join in saying "we believe," we are really saying, "I bet my life on this relationship."

But what are we saying about this God we believe in? Consider the matter this way. Suppose a one-year-old baby could give a logical answer to the question, "Why do you believe your mother loves you?" She would probably say, "I believe she loves me because she holds me close and cuddles me, she comforts me, she feeds me with her very self, she rocks me and sings to me, she tucks me in and watches over me." Verbs, lots of verbs. That is what a deep and lasting relationship is made up of. The creed is also basically verbs of love. Jesus Christ came, suffered, was crucified, died, was buried, descended, rose, ascended, is seated, will come again. Verbs describing what God has done for you and me.

The creed, then, is the story of God's love. The Almighty Father who made us loved us so much that he gave us the freedom to grow as persons, but we got off the track and strayed like lost sheep. So he sent his Son to redeem us (*redeem* means "to make good again"). His Son lived and died and rose again that we might have life in all of its fullness. However, when he ascended, he did not leave us to flounder like helpless orphans and fall back into sin; he gave us his victorious Spirit and banded us together in a company imbued with that Spirit, a company called "the Church," that we might live in his presence now and forever.

There is one other ancient credal statement; it is called the Athanasian Creed. It is identified with Athanasias, bishop of Alexandria, Egypt, in the fourth century. He was a strong and competent defender of the faith; this creed, however, is probably of much later origin. While the Athanasian Creed appears in both the *Lutheran Book of Worship* and the *Book of Common Prayer* it is seldom if ever used in worship. However, it is used on occasion in the Church of England. This creed is only of interest as a historic document, and has no official standing in any American church.

See Redemption, Doctrine, Trinity.

Cross

THE CROSS is the most sacred of all Christian symbols. In ancient times, the cross was the instrument for a lingering and torturous death for offenders against the state. If you had lived in Jesus' time and were a highway robber or had threatened a revolution, or had encouraged a crowd to get out of control, and had been caught, you probably would have been crucified.

Those who schemed to get rid of Jesus could have had him murdered quietly. However, they wanted to have him executed in public, with all the suffering and shame of crucifixion. When you read the story of his Passion in each of the four Gospels, there is no question but that he died "for us and for our salvation," as the creed puts it.

He who died on the Cross rose victorious over death. That is why the Cross is the symbol both of Jesus' death and of his Resurrection. By his death and Resurrection he brought us back to God. So when we look at the Cross and think about our Lord, it is a victory symbol. When we look at the Cross and think about ourselves, it is a forgiveness symbol. That is why the Cross is centrally displayed in churches. That is why the Cross is traced on our foreheads when we are baptized. It is the sign of the new covenant between God and his people. And you and I, members of the Church, are in this new relationship with God.

See Covenant, Resurrection, Salvation.

D

Death

THE DEATH of the body, of course, occurs when physical life leaves it. The Old Testament recognizes the fact that we all die. But the death of Jesus Christ brought about an enormous change in the way Christians think about death. The New Testament teaches us that Christ himself experienced death and in so doing destroyed its power: he rose from the dead. The Resurrection of Christ and our resurrection through faith in him are the great new Christian facts. A Christian does not have to be afraid of death; the sting of death has been removed (1 Cor. 15:55–56). But a Christian must still prepare to meet God, who will see him as he is. Belief in the "resurrection of the body," as we say in the Creed, means that we believe we shall be recognizably and responsibly ourselves beyond the grave.

When a person dies, especially someone you love, you naturally have great sorrow. The Church understands this and does not pretend that it is not so. But it helps you overcome your sorrow by holding up a mighty truth that is even stronger than death. When you go to a funeral there are, of course, prayers for the departed and for those who especially mourn that person's loss, but there is also an underlying and sustaining affirmation of faith in the resurrection — the Resurrection of Christ and ours through faith in him. We hear these or similar words:

> I am the resurrection and the life, says the Lord, he who believes in me, though he die, yet shall he live, and whosoever lives and believes in me shall never die. (John 11:25–26)

> God so loved the world that he gave his Son that whoever believes in him should not perish but have eternal life. (John 3:16)

> Nothing (not even death) shall separate us from the love of God which is in Christ Jesus our Lord. (Rom. 8:39)

> I know that my redeemer lives. (Job 19:25)

This reiterated emphasis on the Resurrection swallows up the bitter pangs of grief. As the Lord promised his disciples the night before his death, "Your sorrow will turn into joy" (John 16:20). He was speaking of that "everlasting joy" about which Isaiah wrote. This is not trivial, shallow joy which has only narrow, worldly horizons. Everlasting joy is grounded in faith in the Heavenly Father's sustaining love and power which causes "sorrow and sighing to flee away" (Isa. 35:11). It is our faith that the dead are alive with him because God keeps all things in his care.

What we believe about God and about Jesus Christ makes all the difference. Not only life but even death takes on new meaning; for in death we are not cut off from God's love. The Lord is our Savior and our Friend both herein and hereafter (John 14:1-4).

See Easter, Grief, Resurrection, Resurrection of the Body.

Devil

THE DEVIL is the personification of evil. In the Bible he is sometimes called Satan, Hebrew for "the adversary," and sometimes Beelzebub which means "the chief devil."

There is so much evil in the world that we naturally think that some powerful being must be in charge of it, like the general of a wicked army. Whatever may be the truth in that, we know that life is an endless battle. The New Testament describes it as a spiritual battle: "We are not contending against flesh and blood, but . . . against the world rulers of this present darkness, against spiritual wickedness in heavenly places" (Eph. 6:12). Our Lord thought of it in these terms also. The Devil represents all the forces of darkness which are seeking to defeat the will of God.

The forces of darkness come into clearer focus when we think of them in terms of Jesus' temptations in the wilderness (Luke 4:1-13; Matt. 4:1-11). Evil is real and potent and personal; no wonder *it* becomes *he*—the adversary, Satan. And what Satan proposes is often something good which has been twisted. Like a car which has been in a wreck and the chassis has been bent—it looks all right, but it isn't. What Satan offered Jesus was not all bad, but it was presented as all good. Satan offered Jesus just what he wanted: the certainty that he could provide for people's needs, that he could have dominion over the kingdoms of the world, and that his faith would not waver. So it is that evil masquerades as good.

There is a Canaanite myth in which the Day Star aspires to the place of the Most High in heaven but is thrown out and falls to the nethermost depths. This story found its way into Isaiah's poetry (Isa. 14:12–15). The Latin for the name "Day Star" is *Lucifer.* So it is that evil which is the almost good and parades as *altogether good* is in truth the *altogether bad.* Lucifer is the fallen angel, "the deceiver of the whole world" who is thrown out of heaven, whose other name is the Devil (Rev. 12:7–9).

This picture of the Devil who works against our better selves is vivid and helps make clear to us the struggle between right and wrong. Who has not been tempted to do what appeared to be right but what was altogether wrong? Gossip and slander are presented as noble truth-telling. Selfishness pretends to be simply the most practical way of handling one's affairs.

As angels represent the agents of God to help us, so demons represent the evil powers that enter into us to plague us. This makes it harder for us to be good. Jesus spoke about casting out devils, and he also described someone as being "bound by Satan." The demons recognized Jesus as their enemy, and he cast them out in God's Name (Mark 5:1–20; Matt. 12:22–32). Through the Cross and Resurrection our Lord proved himself the victor over evil. By his strength we can be victors, too.

See Angels, Evil.

Disciple

A DISCIPLE is one who follows and learns from another person. We usually think of the word *disciple* as referring to twelve of Jesus' followers (known more specifically as apostles) later sent forth in his name. Actually a disciple is anyone who is learning from some other person. If you trust an older person and want to be with and learn from that person, you are his or her disciple. One who is just beginning a profession in law or medicine or architecture may become the apprentice of a person of recognized stature in that field. Supreme Court Justice Sandra Day O'Connor selects from a list of applicants the most promising young lawyers who have graduated in recent years to be her clerks. This is regarded as a great honor because those young lawyers can be with Justice O'Connor and learn from her—as her disciples.

In Palestine in biblical times a young person often went to a rabbi and became his disciple. To become disciples of Jesus the Twelve left their families and businesses and homes and followed him. They learned his teachings, and perhaps what was even more important, they lived with him and learned from his example. At least one man declined an invitation from Jesus to become his disciple (see the story of the rich young man, Matt. 19:16–22). Jesus chose the Twelve from a large number of his disciples—we do not know how many, but we do know that the group included women (Luke 6:12–13; 8:1–3).

Every Christian is a disciple of Jesus because we learn from him and try to follow him.

See Apostle, Layperson, Ministry.

Discipline

DISCIPLINE is training which strengthens and corrects. We usually think of discipline as a way of maintaining order and often as punishment. It is more than these.

A discipline is a program of learning which helps you make a branch of knowledge or a skill your own. Bjorn Borg, unsurpassed professional tennis player of the late 1970s, used to run twelve miles and practice tennis four hours every day. That discipline built up his stamina and perfected his tennis skill; it made him into a superb player. The same discipline of practice and training is engaged in by an accomplished musician or by an athletic team. A polished writer was once asked how he did it. He replied, "Nothing I produce is ever just written. It is rewritten and rewritten and rewritten."

Another purpose of discipline is to put a person back on track so that a necessary job can get done. The purpose of order in the classroom, for example, is to let the class do its work. There is no point in having a group of people sitting around quietly for the sake of sitting around quietly.

The purpose of punishment is to help those who get out of line get back in line. Real discipline must result in self-discipline if it is to work. We cannot always have other people telling us what to do and correcting us when we are wrong. Our instructors, whether they are teachers in the classroom or supervisors on the job, try to help us learn skills so that we can use them ourselves when they are called for. A self-disciplined person is able to know when to use a skill and how to use it without being told.

Paul writes about discipline in 1 Corinthians 9:24–27.

See Disciple, Lent.

Doctrine

DOCTRINE is teaching. The doctrine of the Church is its teaching, the body of truths its members believe. A dogma is a specific teaching of the Church which is of primary importance. The Incarnation— the belief that God came into the world in the person Jesus—is an established Christian dogma.

A thinking person is likely to ask, "Who determines what is in the body of truths Christians believe?" The classic summary statements of Christian belief are the Apostles' and Nicene Creeds. These attained their authoritative stature in different ways.

Through the centuries there have been other summary statements of Christian belief. One such is the *Didache,* an anonymous Christian treatise of the second century A.D. Its full English title is *The Teachings of the Twelve Apostles.* But neither this nor any other has the authority that Christians the world over give to the Apostles' and Nicene Creeds.

See Creed.

E

Ecumenical Movement/Ecumenism

ECUMENICAL means general or universal, that which pertains to the whole Christian church in the broadest sense. The Ecumenical movement which began back in the 1800s involves Christians of many denominations in striving for unity. In recent decades we can see the results of ecumenism in the work of the Consultation on Church Union (COCU) among a number of non-Roman Catholic churches in the United States, the Second Vatican Council of the Roman church, and several ongoing dialogues between Roman Catholics and other churches. The results have been inter-denominational efforts to develop areas of mutual concern and to define Christian belief in terms ultimately acceptable to all parties, looking toward the eventual reunion of Christendom.

Thoughtful Christians are haunted and challenged by our Lord's prayer for his disciples "that they may all be one . . . so that the world may believe that thou hast sent me" (John 17:21). They labor to fulfill the desire of the Good Shepherd that "there shall be one flock under one shepherd" (John 10:16).

Eschatology

ESCHATOLOGY is the teaching about last things—the end of history. God is the Lord of history, of its beginning and of its end, the end of the world.

This is all tied up with the belief in the Second Coming of Christ. (The Greek word for his Second Coming is *parousia*.)

God's purposes were revealed in Jesus Christ; the Kingdom of God was a present reality in all that he said and did and was. However, the ultimate fulfillment of God's purposes, the coming of his kingdom in its fulness, will not take place until Christ returns in power and glory at the end of history.

Because all human activity and history will be assessed in the light of God's purposes as revealed in Christ, the Lord's Second

Coming will be a time of judgment. The conflicts between good and evil in history will be overcome. The love of God revealed in Jesus Christ will be victorious over sin and all the powers of evil.

The Eternal Judge is not to be thought of as merciless and tyrannical. The Fourth Gospel gives us a better way to think about the matter: "This is the judgment, that the light has come into the world, and men loved darkness rather than light because their deeds were evil" (John 3:19). The Eternal Judge is the Risen Lord; "He will come again in glory to judge the living and the dead, and his kingdom will have no end," we say in the Nicene Creed. There is reassuring good news related to the Last Judgment: he who is the Judge knows firsthand what it is like to be a human being. He sympathizes with our weaknesses for in every respect he has been tempted as we are, yet without sin (Heb. 4:15). So because he has suffered and been tempted he will be understanding and merciful (Heb. 2:17–18).

The symbols of that final wrap-up day are eternal life and the Kingdom of God. These can be thought of as our ultimate fulfillment both as individuals and as a community of believers. It will be a time when the best of all possibilities for individuals will be realized, and a time when life together under God will achieve that ideal state of which we caught a glimpse in Jesus' teaching about the Kingdom and in his works of healing and forgiving.

See Eternal Life, Kingdom of God.

Eternal Life

ETERNAL LIFE has more to do with the quality and essence of life than it does with endless existence.

When you are with someone you love very much, you have little awareness of time; it really doesn't matter. You are having a *good* time. Being with God is something of the same experience; the Bible calls it eternal life. This does not necessarily mean that you are thinking about God or saying your prayers or sitting in church, although these things may be part of it. Frederick Buechner, a provocative Christian writer, has described being "with God" as being similar to the situation where we say someone is "with it," that is, completely caught up in what one is doing, totally one's self, totally free. We describe that infectiously wonderful state of being as "cloud nine"; it is paradise. At such a time the person who is "with it" has life in all of its fulness.

We tend to think of eternal life as something endless which begins when this life is over. Rather, think of it as what happens when life truly begins. The New Testament challenges us to think of eternal life in this way: "Lay hold on eternal life to which you were called" (1 Tim. 6:12). Jesus was talking about the same thing. "I am come," he said, "that they may have life in all of its abundance" (John 10:10). He had it; he intends for us to have it also.

So to live eternal life in all of its wonderfulness is to be with our Heavenly Father as the Lord was with Him, and with each other as our Lord is with us, this side of the grave and beyond.

See Eschatology.

Eucharist

THE HOLY EUCHARIST is the family meal of the people of God. It has a variety of other names; among them are the Lord's Supper, Holy Communion, the Divine Liturgy, and the Mass.

At the Last Supper the night before he died, Jesus interpreted his approaching death and Resurrection by taking and blessing and breaking bread, and by pouring out wine. He not only gave this bread and wine to his disciples, he also directed them to have a similar holy meal "in remembrance of me" (Luke 22:19) after he was gone. In the Eucharist we repeat his fourfold action—we take bread, bless it, break it, and give it to each other—in thankful remembrance of his life and death for our salvation, and of his Resurrection which overcame the power of death for us. For some the vivid retelling of the Lord's sacrifice and death in the Eucharist is the reenacting of that event; for others the Eucharist is a reverent remembrance of that event. Basically, the Eucharist is a foretaste of the heavenly banquet that we shall share with our Lord and with all faithful people.

Bread is the universally common food. And in many countries wine is still the common drink; no other drink is safe. So the bread and wine used in the Eucharist stand for the food and drink without which we could not live. In bringing them forward as our offering for use in this service they represent our life and labor. The wheat and grapes are the result of human effort in cooperation with God the Creator. Think how many people are involved before these gifts of God were brought to the service—farmers, manufacturers, shippers, merchants; truly the life and labor of society are represented in them, and all this is presented to God.

At the high point in the service (variously called the Prayer of Consecration, the Great Thanksgiving, the Canon of the Mass) the bread and wine are consecrated, that is, they are set apart as holy. Then we receive them back, but radically changed. They are sometimes called the "Holy Mysteries." They have been blessed and sanctified by the Holy Spirit that they may be for us holy food, the Body and Blood of Jesus Christ our Lord. The meaning here has been interpreted differently by theologians but Christians agree that in the Eucharist the faithful are strengthened and sustained by the Lord's life and Spirit in order to go forth to serve him in the everyday world. So it is that a common meal is transformed into a holy meal.

Earlier in the Eucharist we seek God's forgiveness for our sins against him and our neighbors. (The latter becomes graphic in many churches when the Peace—the greeting of those around us in Christ's name—is exchanged.) The fact that we are invited in the Name of the Lord to come to his Table and the fact that we come shoulder to shoulder, with our fellow Christians to share broken bread, is a striking symbol of forgiveness and reconciliation. Truly, Christ is our peace and has through his sacrifice broken down the wall of hostility which separated us from one another and from God (Eph. 2:13–16).

The Holy Eucharist strengthens us for service in Christ's Name, and at the conclusion we are sent forth into the world to love and serve the Lord.

See Consecration, Mission, The Peace, Sacrament, Sacrifice, Witness.

Evil

EVIL is the name we apply to that which is morally reprehensible. It is the absolute opposite of good.

When we say something is "bad" we usually mean that it misses the mark, is below standard. We apply the term to people as well as things. There is the unexpressed suggestion that improvement is a possibility. We say, "It can be fixed." Or of people we say, "He is a bad youngster, but under the right influence, I think he would straighten up."

But the word *evil* has a very different meaning. It always applies to a person. No one would describe his automobile as "evil." He would say, "I have a lemon," meaning that it is prone to mechanical failures. Only persons are evil, nefarious, diabolical. Such reprehensible individuals are not thought of as being merely on the wrong track and possibly subject to conversion to a better way of life. They are thoroughly wicked. The Damned.

Such baseness of character surely must have a model and source of inspiration. Enter the Devil. Wickedness is so universal; there has to be someone who exercises diabolical command. The New Testament speaks of "spiritual wickedness in high places" (Eph. 6:12). And those who are under the power of this darkness are "the children of the Devil."

See Devil.

Exorcism

EXORCISM is the process of expelling evil spirits. Jesus often exercised this power. When confronted by persons afflicted by demons, Jesus would command those evil spirits to leave their victim (Luke 4:31-36, 40-41). When he sent the Twelve apostles out to preach the gospel of the kingdom in surrounding villages he gave them the power both to cast out demons (or unclean spirits) and to heal in his Name (Luke 9:1-2; Matt. 10:1, 5; Mark 6:7). The writers of the Gospels saw in this power of Jesus over evil spirits concrete evidence of the power of God over evil and evidence that in the person of Jesus the Kingdom of God was a present reality.

See Devil, Evil.

F

Faith

FAITH is the response of a person to someone that person trusts.

A few years ago there was a billboard that featured a picture of a child's hand holding that of an adult (as a little girl would hold the hand of her father while crossing the street). Above it was the one word: "Confidence"; it was an insurance company ad. Confidence means faith. The little child places her faith in her father; she believes he will protect her from the dangers of the traffic. She has to do the walking, but she is confident he will get her safely to the other side.

Most of us experienced the same need for trust when we learned to swim. As soon as you get over your fear that you will sink and learn to trust the water to hold you up, you can swim and even float!

The author of the Letter to the Hebrews defined faith as "the assurance of things hoped for, the conviction of things not seen" (Heb. 11:1). How often our Lord speaks of the need to have faith. Read what he says and substitute the word *expectancy* for *faith*, and its meaning becomes clearer. Here is an example:

> As Jesus passed . . . two blind men followed him, crying aloud, "Have mercy on us, Son of David." When he entered the house the blind men came to him; and Jesus said to them, "Do you believe that I am able to do this?" They said to him, "Yes, Lord." Then he touched their eyes, saying, "According to your faith [expectancy] be it done to you." And their eyes were opened. (Matt. 9:27–30)

It is not always easy to have faith in God. When we are overcome by a sense of our unworthiness, perhaps we have cheated somebody or lacked the courage to tell the truth or been mean out of spite — it is hard to believe that God still loves us. Yet we live by our faith in his merciful goodness. We have faith that our Heavenly Father is as loving and forgiving of the penitent and as understanding as Jesus was in the Gospels. Our confidence is in Him, for as Jesus said, "He that has seen me has seen the Father" (John 12:45). The Christian lives by faith.

Sometimes the word *faith* is used in another way: we speak of "the faith," meaning that body of belief to which we give assent as Christians.

The Fall

THE FALL is the term used to describe our separation from God. God created us to live in companionship with him. He intended that this should be the fullest and happiest kind of relationship. But the terrible truth is that people are not living that way. Another fact is that by our own efforts we simply cannot recreate that God-intended relationship.

The Bible calls this "the Fall" and tells it in a story in the Book of Genesis (3:1–24). Here an ancient Jewish writer is telling in a story the facts that he knows to be true about himself, about all of us. The story says that at first man and woman lived in a beautiful garden (that is, in complete happiness) and in perfect relationship with God. Then, because they chose to disobey a rule which God had made to protect their happiness, they found themselves separated from God (exiled from the garden) and unable to get back. It was because of their self-centeredness. As the popular song puts it, "I did it my way." But, as the Bible makes clear, "my way" is not God's way, it is sin.

Whatever you may question of the details of the story, it gives a true picture of you and me and every other person who has lived in the world – except Jesus Christ, God's Son, who though tempted as we are was without sin. All of us, except our Lord, have to be brought back to God. The story of the Fall, then, is about three things: (1) God made us to be happy with him; (2) we are separated from him by sin, not only our own actual sins but the sinfulness of the whole human race; (3) only God can bring about our reconciliation (2 Cor. 5:19).

The gospel is the story of how this reconciliation takes place. Paul put it this way: "The gospel is the power of God for salvation to everyone who has faith" (Rom. 1:16). Christ gives us his Spirit and lets us take our place in his family of faith-filled folk, the Christian church. So our relationship with God is restored, and the Church is the company of penitent and forgiven sinners.

See Salvation, Sin.

Fasting

FASTING is the ancient and universal religious discipline of going without food. It is not confined to Christianity or to ancient Judaism, from which the Christian practice derives. It is a discipline transferring one's attention from physical to spiritual needs, from feeding the body to feeding the soul. Fasts are observed in varying degrees. In an extreme form fasting means going without food altogether, or perhaps allowing one's self only bread and water. The length of time—from one meal to several days—varies depending on the occasion and the intention. Closely related to fasting is the discipline of abstinence, which means abstaining from a particular food, such as meat. The principal fast days for Christians are Ash Wednesday and Good Friday.

Lenten fasting is observed as a reminder of the suffering our Lord underwent for us. This is best done as inobtrusively as possible, certainly not jokingly. Every time we desire that normally enjoyed food or drink—or whatever else—should become a devotional moment in which to thank the Lord Christ for his great love in giving his life for us.

See Church Year, Discipline.

Fear of God

THE FEAR OF GOD is the deep-seated human attitude toward manifestations of divine presence and power; it is an emotional mixture of amazement and wonder, of reverence and awe, as well as of trepidation. We are so in the habit of emphasizing the love of God that we overlook this significant biblical theme.

In the Old Testament, Uzzah is killed when he casually touches the Ark of God (2 Sam. 6:1-7). One doesn't take lightly coming in contact with the holy. Jacob wrestles with an unknown stranger in the dark, and when he realizes he has had an encounter with God his awed reaction is, "I have seen God face to face, and yet my life is preserved" (Gen. 32:30). Moses at the burning bush covered his face "for he was afraid to look at God" (Exod. 3:6).

In the New Testament, when God (or his angel messenger) makes himself known, he liberates believers from fear. To Mary, the angel said, "Do not be afraid, Mary, for you have found favor with God" (Luke 1:30). The angel's first words to the shepherds were, "Be not afraid, for behold, I bring you good tidings of great joy which shall be to all the people" (Luke 2:10). And all through Jesus' ministry when people became aware of the immeasurable distance which separated them from the living God as manifested in Jesus, fear joined hands with astonishment. Notice the reaction of the disciples when Jesus calms the storm: "They were filled with awe and said to one another, 'Who then is this, that even the wind and the sea obey him?'" (Mark 4:41). When Jesus raised the son of the widow of Nain to life, "fear seized them all and they glorified God" (Luke 7:16). In the Gospels this natural human reaction of awesome wonder is coupled with a sign of faith, however fleeting. When Jesus healed the paralytic, "amazement seized them all, and they glorified God and were filled with awe, saying, 'We have seen strange things today'" (Luke 5:26). At the time of the Transfiguration, that occasion when Jesus was revealed to the disciples as God's Son, the three disciples on the mountain with Jesus heard the voice from heaven (i.e., the voice of God), "they fell on their faces and were filled with awe. But Jesus came and touched them, saying, 'Rise, and have no fear'" (Matt. 17:6–7). And the angel at the empty tomb reassured the women with, "Fear not, you seek Jesus who was crucified" (Matt. 28:5). The fear of God is a continual thread throughout the gospel account.

Fear is also a recognized part of human reaction in the presence of manifestations of divine power in the life of the early Church. As a result of the preaching of Peter on the Jewish feast of Pentecost when the Holy Spirit came upon the apostles, "fear came upon every soul; and many wonders and signs were done through the apostles" (Acts 2:43). Paul helps transform this natural human reaction of fear and fright when he writes to his Christian comrades, "You did not receive the spirit of slavery to fall back into fear, but you have received the spirit of sonship. When we cry, 'Abba, Father,' it is the Spirit himself bearing witness with our spirit that we are children of God" (Rom. 8:15–16).

Throughout the New Testament members of the Church are called those who "fear the Lord," and so Luke can record, "The church throughout all Judea and Gallilee and Samaria had peace and was built up; and walking in the fear of the Lord and, in the comfort of the Holy Spirit, it was multiplied" (Acts 9:31).

See Awe.

Flesh

FLESH is a frequently used biblical term for the human in contrast to the divine, and for things material as opposed to things spiritual. It is the basic element that distinguishes humanity from God.

Here are examples of the ways in which the term is used.

- It refers to all humanity: "Let all flesh bless his holy Name for ever and ever" (Ps. 145:21).
- It is a poetic term for "a human being": "The Word became flesh and dwelt among us" (John 1:14).
- Sometimes it refers to living creatures generally: "The glory of the Lord shall be revealed, and all flesh shall see it together" (Isa. 40:5).
- The word is also used to describe the physical and animal nature of human beings in contrast to their moral and spiritual nature: "The desires of the flesh are against the Spirit. . . . these are opposed to each other" (Gal. 5:17).
- The term may also be used simply to describe our physicalness: "The spirit indeed is willing but the flesh is weak" (Mark 14:38).
- In spite of its material nature, flesh is sometimes thought of as capable of transcending the merely physical: "My heart and my flesh rejoice in the living God" (Ps. 84:2).

These are the principal meanings of the word *flesh* in the Bible.

All of these uses refer to different aspects of humanness. All of us know firsthand about the limitations, the fallibility, and our proneness to wrongdoing because we are flesh and blood. The amazingly wonderful Christian belief is that God's Son would come to us in this way.

See Incarnation.

Forgiveness

FORGIVENESS is that extraordinary act by the offended one which makes everything right again between that person and the offender. Christian forgiveness is first about how God restores our relationship with him, and then about how we restore relationships with those who have hurt us.

We begin to appreciate how great a thing forgiveness is when we think about it in money terms. Jesus told a parable about the servant of a king whose debt to his lord amounted to more than the wages a laborer could earn in fifteen years – a tremendous sum! In response to his pleas for mercy his master forgave him the debt, wiped it out. But the heartless fellow went out and jumped on a fellow worker who owed him the equivalent of one day's wage and showed him no mercy. His lord, when he heard what had taken place, punished the ungrateful servant severely (Luke 18:23–35).

Our sins are in God's sight like the monumental debt of the king's servant and the ways in which others have hurt or offended us are as trivial in comparison as the small amount owed that servant. This throws light on Matthew's version of the Lord's Prayer: "Forgive us our debts, as we also have forgiven our debtors" (Matt. 6:12).

Forgiveness then is cancelling a debt, putting an end to an unhappy situation created by our violation of the rights of another. A neighbor forgives the boys whose baseball broke her window. A high school student forgives a friend whose failure to speak up allows unpleasant gossip to keep her out of the school play. The fault is still there; forgiveness does not deny the fault as though it did not exist. Restitution still has to be made. The window has to be fixed, the truth told. But the relationship with the offended has been restored.

Forgiveness is not easy. God in Christ has offered us forgiveness, restoring us to the status of his loving and faithful children. The cost was high: Christ died on the cross for us. We cannot really appreciate this divine graciousness unless we have practiced forgiveness ourselves and felt the hurt that forgiving involves. That is why in the Sermon on the Mount the Lord's Prayer is followed by this comment:

> For if you forgive men their trespasses, your heavenly Father also will forgive you; but if you do not forgive men their trespasses, neither will your Father forgive your trespasses. (Matt. 6:14–15)

Jesus Christ lived as a man and died on the cross so that we might know how God's love reaches out to us, no matter what we do. He loves us, even when we are hateful and selfish and mean, and he gives us the courage to ask for and receive forgiveness.

See Atonement, Justification, Reconciliation.

Fundamentalism

FUNDAMENTALISM is a term used in religious circles to describe belief in the literal verbal accuracy of the book which is basic to that religion's belief and practice. For Moslem fundamentalists the book is the Koran, for Christian fundamentalists it is the Bible, for orthodox Jews the Hebrew scriptures.

Christian fundamentalists believe that every word in the Bible is literally true—the inspired Word of God. The Bible is seen not only as the indisputable authority in faith and morals; it is also a literal historical record.

This point of view developed in the early part of the twentieth century among American Protestants as a reaction to liberal theological interpretations of the Bible, which fundamentalists thought were watering down the Bible's meaning and message. The Bible as the Word of God is, they asserted, unquestionably accurate regardless of what science or philosophy or scholarly research might say to the contrary. This stand sets up antipathy between science and religion. For example, the Bible states that the world was created in six days; the theory of evolution says it took millions of years. For the nonfundamentalist, this supposed contradiction is explained by pointing out that the Bible and science are not dealing with the same question. The Bible is a religious document and says that God created the world and found his creation good. Science is not concerned with what God did or does, but rather with *how* this world came into existence. Scientists are interested in the process, not in who is ultimately behind the process.

The fundamentalist is obliged though to support the Bible's statement as scientific truth. For the fundamentalist should a single word or concept in the Bible be deemed false then all of its contents will be subjected to question and disbelief. Similar to a house of cards, where if one is removed the whole house is destroyed, the authority of Scripture rests on the inerrancy of every detail.

See Bible, Creation.

G

Glossolalia

GLOSSOLALIA is an ecstatic kind of praying in incomprehensible speech. The practice originated in the early Christian church, then largely disappeared, but has in modern times been practiced by Pentecostal sects and more recently by groups in mainline churches. It is also called "speaking in tongues" or the "gift of tongues" and is an evidence of having been baptized by the Holy Spirit. It was evidently a practice in the Church in Corinth in the days of the Apostle Paul, for he writes to them at some length about it. See 1 Corinthians 14:6–19. While Paul admitted to speaking in tongues himself, he was somewhat skeptical about its value in public worship. His conclusion was, "In church I would rather speak five words with my mind, in order to instruct others, then ten thousand words in a tongue."

See Charismatic Christian.

God

GOD is the one Supreme Being, the creator and ruler of the universe. The ancient Israelite could not rationally explain the God he believed in. He could only say, "This has been my experience of him and that of my forebears," and then he would enumerate events in the history of his people. See Psalms 78, 105, 106, and 136. We, like the Israelites of old, believe in God because we experience his presence and power, not because we argue about his existence. We take our images and ideas of God from Scripture.

In the Old Testament we learn that God created us and all the world—planets and grasshoppers, rivers and peacocks, mountains and horses, and people—you and me. Everything had a beginning and that beginning was God; "In the beginning God" are the Bible's opening words. And God chose the Israelites to be "his people," delivered them from Egyptian slavery, gave them the Ten Commandments by which to live, and gave them a homeland. So God reveals himself: there is only one God, and he is a caring, moral God. In the course of their history the Israelites came to realize that God is also holy, just, compassionate, merciful, loving; such were the insights of the prophets of the eighth and seventh centuries before Christ.

The New Testament opens with a wonderful truth: God sends his Son into the world in the person of Jesus of Nazareth. "The Word became flesh and dwelt among us, full of grace and truth," says John's Gospel, and he goes on to explain, "No one has seen God; the only Son, who is in the bosom of the Father, he has made him known" (John 1:14, 18). And before his earthly story is finished Jesus has died on the Cross and we come to realize that God loves us so much that, in the person of his Son, he is willing to suffer and die for us, his headstrong, erring children, in order to bring us back into fellowship with him. Then God raises our Lord from the dead and bestows his victorious Spirit on the company of believers, and so the Christian church is born.

The invisible God has made himself known to us as our Creator, our Savior from sin, and our Sustainer through his Spirit in the life of the Church; three manifestations of the one holy God. The Holy Trinity we call it.

See Church, Creation, Creed, Incarnation, Trinity.

Godparents

GODPARENTS or sponsors make the promises and enter into the Baptismal Covenant in baptism for an infant being baptized. The custom is said to have started in the very early days of Christian persecution when being a Christian was a precarious business and the natural parents might not survive to raise their child as a Christian; one's godparents would take over that responsibility. In later less turbulent times godparents have been considered their child's special Christian friends. They have none of the responsibilities of parents—to raise, train, and discipline their children, as well as to love and care for them. The only responsibility of godparents is to be their godchild's Christian friend and his or her example of what it is like to be a Christian.

Being a child's godparent can develop into a wonderful relationship. One lady spends a whole day with her godchild every year doing whatever that child wants to do from the moment they first meet in the morning until late in the afternoon. "Through the years we've been sightseeing at the zoo, the airport, and even a TV studio," she says. "We have eaten pizzas together, licked each other's ice cream cones, and laughed a lot." Think of the confidences that are exchanged between friends like that! A godparent might help a child get a summer job, or act as a trusted adviser about colleges, jobs, and other matters.

Here is a privilege to be enjoyed as well as a responsibility.

See Baptism.

Golgotha

GOLGOTHA is the Arabic form of the Hebrew word meaning "skull." It is the name of the place where Jesus was crucified. In the Vulgate, the Bible of the Roman Catholics, the Latin word used is *calvaria* meaning "a bare skull." The translators of the King James Version of the Bible made *calvaria* part of a proper name—"Mount Calvary" that only appears in the Bible once (Luke 23:33). The exact location of Mount Calvary is not known. It was probably a slight rise in the ground of about eighteen feet, a stony area which at the time of the Lord's Crucifixion was just outside the wall around Jerusalem.

Gospel

A GOSPEL is good news; the Christian gospel is the good news about Jesus Christ. The Greek word *evaggelion* means "good news." It comes into English via two routes. By transliteration it is lifted over into English as *evangel* and the writer of a gospel is an evangelist. It was also translated into Old English—*godspell*—which in time became *gospel*.

An evangelist is not a court reporter nor is he a newspaper correspondent sending out wire dispatches from the scene. He is recording the good news about Jesus Christ as he understands it.

He uses the materials which have come to him in the way and in the order in which they will enhance, explain, and convince his readers of the wonderful news contained in the life and teachings, the death and Resurrection of Jesus Christ. A gospel is proclamation, not biography; the writer is declaring his conviction about his subject.

The evangelists who wrote the four Gospels each had a somewhat different view of who Jesus was. Matthew views him as the One who fulfills Hebrew Scripture. To Mark, he is the Son of God and a lonely warrior. Luke presents him as the compassionate Lord. And Jesus in the Gospel of John is the eternal King.

Most of the material each evangelist had before him when he wrote his gospel has no dateline—there was no indication when the saying or the episode occurred in the course of Jesus' ministry. Therefore, each writer arranged his material in the way in which it would best tell the story of Jesus as he understood it. That is why, for instance, the cleansing of the Temple by Jesus occurs at the beginning of Holy Week in Luke but in John's Gospel it is one of the first events in Jesus' ministry (Luke 19:45–46; John 2:13–22).

What makes these writings good news is the fact that they make clear that God in the person of Jesus Christ cares about each of us and loves us. He does not just love us when we are good but even when we are bad and unlovely, that is, sinful. While he hates the sin he loves the sinner. We see this great truth in the way Jesus treated people, in the parables he told, and especially in the way he died, offering his life in love for others. God is as loving and forgiving as was Jesus, and he is like that toward each one of us; that is the good news, the gospel each of the four evangelists has recorded. Paul's way of putting it was, "God shows his love for us in that while we were yet sinners Christ died for us" (Rom. 5:8).

Grace

THE GRACE OF GOD is his freely given, saving power at work in the world and in us. Grace has been called "God's fairy godmother characteristic." What the fairy godmother did for Cinderella was infinitely more than she could have earned or demanded; it just unbelievably happened . . . for free!

We can think of God's grace in at least three ways:

First, we see God's grace at work in the Old Testament when he selects the Israelites to be his chosen people. It was not because they had done wonderful things and were deserving, but just because he loved them. Having chosen them, he firmly refused to give them up. Bad as they were at times, God loved them so much that he would not give up his plan for them. He had made a covenant (an agreement) with them, and the covenant itself was an act of grace. Through the years God's grace continued to be offered to his people in spite of their disobedience.

The second meaning of grace is familiar to us in the words "the grace of our Lord Jesus Christ." God shows his special love and favor to us through all that Jesus Christ said and did, and all that happened to him. This meaning lies behind the words, "The Word became flesh and dwelt among us, full of grace and truth; we have beheld his glory, glory as of the only Son from the Father" (John 1:14).

Since Jesus died on the Cross and rose from the dead, the grace of God is plainer than ever before. It shows the depth and wonder of God's love—the same love of the same God who had chosen Israel and had been so patient through the long years before Christ came. In Jesus Christ we see the special love and favor God has toward us.

The third meaning of God's grace is that his love and kindness are working inwardly in our hearts. By God's grace we are given power to act in ways acceptable to him. In many of our prayers we ask God to give us grace to resist temptation and to do his will. These are prayers for God's power, for his Spirit, to work through our lives. Sometimes God's grace is known to us through the love and help of people around us. The church you attend with its worship and fellowship is one place where this can take place. One of the chief ways in which God gives us indwelling power is through the sacraments. That is why they are called the "means of grace."

See Covenant, Sacrament.

Grief

GRIEF is keen mental suffering because of the loss of a loved one or friend. Mourning gives expression to grief. Mourning evolves; grief is constant. Mourning has a varied wardrobe; grief never changes clothes.

The mourner agonizingly relives the last days and weeks of the loved one's life: *"If I had only done this or that she would still be alive."* Often the mourner feels guilty and self-reproachful: *"I could have been more thoughtful"*; *"I should have visited her more often."* Sometimes the mourner is reproachful and unappreciative: *"The doctor could have done more; he should have gotten a second opinion."* The mourner can torture him or herself.

But then the mourner comes to the burial service. It is really an Easter celebration. There is a pervading joy because our Christian conviction is that the Risen Christ welcomes our loved one home: "All that the Father gives me will come to me; and him who comes to me I will not cast out" (John 6:37). The mourner's sorrow begins to turn into joy—everlasting joy—and his sadness and sighing begin to flee away.

Grief parts company from mourning at this point. The departed loved one had a distinct and definite place in his or her world and now that place is empty. Here is a somewhat similar experience. Years ago there was a great shade tree at a certain intersection on the Post Road in southern Connecticut. Progress cut it down. To me there was a hole in the sky at that intersection that nothing could fill. Months slipped by but every time I passed that way there was still a hole in the sky at that intersection.

There is a lady whose husband died several years ago; they were very close. Recently she said, "They say it gets better with time. What I want to know is when, when is that going to happen?"

Grief is not self-pity or resentment or a desire to turn back the clock. There is still a hearty participation on All Saints' Day when we thankfully remember "our dearest and our best" who share in "a life of perfect service in God's heavenly kingdom." But there is a certain loneliness which does not quickly depart.

H

Halo

A HALO is special illumination around and above the head of a divine or sacred personage. It is an atmosphere of glory and majesty and sanctity.

Fire and brightness are associated with the presence of God, for example, Moses at the burning bush and the awesome happenings at Mount Sinai at the time of the giving of the Ten Commandments (Exod. 3:2-6; 19:18). The New Testament similarly notes there were "tongues as of fire" on the day of Pentecost (Acts 2:3). So God's presence with special people—Jesus and the saints—is noted by what appears to be the presence of fire behind them which creates a halo.

Heaven

HEAVEN is our name for the wonderful place beyond the grave which our Heavenly Father has prepared for his children. Imaginative persons in the Bible and throughout the age have described in detail what they envision heaven to be like; but in every case it is *their* picture, not everyone's. As theologian Renée Haynes wrote, "The more detailed pictures of life after death are, the less acceptable they seem to be." I think all of us will be surprised when the time comes.

Perhaps the best biblical description is this: "Behold, the dwelling of God is with men. He will dwell with them, and they shall be his people, and God himself will be with them; he will wipe away every tear from their eyes" (Rev. 21:3-4).

You supply the details you would consider sublime. You may find that poetry, or painting, or music whets your heavenly meditation—fuels your dream of paradise.

In any case, being with God will be enough. God as he has shown himself to us in Jesus Christ. He is perfect love and he will lead us in the adventure of life in all of its glorious abundance.

See Resurrection.

Hell

HELL is the name we give to the place in which people find themselves when they have locked themselves out from God and from others. The pictorial descriptions of Hell in the Bible describe unending fire and similar torments (Luke 16:22–24; Rev. 14:9–10). It is a way of saying that because God made us to live with him, now and hereafter, it must be a terribly painful thing to be without his friendship forever. We have a taste of hell even now when we pull into our shell and sulk and refuse to make up after a quarrel. In Dante's *Inferno* the nethermost depths of hell are that place where individuals are frozen in ice, unable to have the companionship of any other person.

Here on earth, people are free to live for themselves, concerned only with their own pleasure; they can turn their backs on the rest of the world as long as they can stand it. They believe that one can do the same thing in the hereafter. This is really what it means to make damned fools of ourselves.

And yet, since God in Christ loves us, he will keep on loving us no matter what we do to ourselves and others. Our Lord said, "Be penitent, and pray believing." So surely the love which will not let us go, the love which we see in Jesus, continually reaches out to us, whatever our situation. As the Psalmist put it, "If I make my bed in Sheol [the place of the departed], thou art there!" (Ps. 139:8).

Hell results from the worst we can do to ourselves. The Good News of Scripture is that the loving Father of us all will never let that be the last word should we turn and repent.

See Eschatology, Savior.

Heresy

HERESY is an opinion which is at variance with the orthodox or accepted doctrine (teaching) of the Church. For example, there was an early Christian heresy called Arianism which contended that Jesus was an unusually noble person but was not God's Son, was not divine. The Council of Nicea in A.D. 325 rejected this belief and produced the Nicene Creed which emphasized over and over the belief in the Lord's divinity as well as belief in his humanity. So the

Church made it clear that Jesus Christ was believed to be unquestionably divine as well as being fully human. Arianism was declared to be heretical.

There was a day when heretics were burned at the stake. Fortunately, we now leave such gruesome practice to television stories.

What should the thinking person do when he or she finds certain orthodox beliefs are difficult to accept? There are at least two options.

First, it is all right to have doubts. Questions and doubts are the growing pains of the mind. But do not have a closed mind. The poet William Cowper was right, "Blind unbelief is sure to err." Be willing to investigate and accept new ideas.

Suppose one has serious doubts about a central Christian teaching such as the Resurrection. Investigate: What is that teaching trying to say? What does it mean? How was it arrived at? Sit down and discuss the matter with one whose Christian commitment you have great respect for—your minister or priest, or an older friend.

Sometime back a middle-aged man went to his priest with the question, "Why do *you* believe in the Resurrection?" Notice this was man to man; he was not seeking the overpowering authority of the Church. After a frank and open discussion the inquirer said, "Why hasn't someone told me this before?" He had used his doubt as a means of growth from possible heresy to profound Christian conviction.

There is another possibility. While the preponderance of possibility lies with the orthodox view, there is always the chance that God's Spirit working through some individual may be nudging the Church into a broader view. The heretic may be standing up for some truth orthodoxy has not yet come to accept (e.g., when Galileo claimed that the world is round, not flat). Such a person has a lonely, often painful, vocation and is only likely to be appreciated in retrospect.

Defenders of the faith and every serious Christian believer need to be open to the Lord's promise, "When the Spirit of truth is come he will lead you into all truth" (John 16:13).

Holy

HOLY characterizes God just as "human" characterizes people. It has been said that holiness is what describes God-ness. As Reginald Heber's hymn puts it:

Holy, holy, holy, Lord God Almighty! . . .
Only thou art holy; there is none beside thee.

You may sometimes think that God is not loving or fair, but if you should think he is not holy, him of whom you speak is no longer God. When we speak of anything else as being holy we are saying that there is something about it which has God's mark upon it. Times, places, things, and people are called "holy" when there is a certain sanctity about them which is easily recognized. They are set apart as sacred.

Holiness is purity and goodness at white-hot intensity. I once saw a lumberyard burn. The heat of the fire was so intense that it caused row after row of stacked lumber suddenly to burst into flame. The prophet says of the "Lord my God, my Holy One" that he is "of purer eyes than to behold evil and canst not look on wrong" for if he did, it would be instantly consumed (Heb. 1:12–13), just as was the lumber in that fire. That is what the holiness of God tries to convey.

See God, Holy Spirit.

Holy Spirit

THE HOLY SPIRIT is the third person of the Trinity and is God as we experience him in the life of the Church and in our lives and those of others. God's Spirit inspired and spoke through the prophets of the Old Testament. Jesus Christ was solely embued with this same Spirit of God (Mark 1:10–11; Luke 4:1–2, 14; John 7:39). After he has risen from the dead the Lord bestowed the Holy Spirit on his faithful followers (John 20:22; Acts 1:8; 2:1–4).

This becomes clear when we realize that after the Lord's Resurrection the disciples, assembled in his Name, became aware of a Spirit in their midst which was like that which they had known when Jesus was physically present with them. They called it "the

Lord's Spirit," or "the Holy Spirit." John's Gospel says that this experience first took place on the evening of the first Easter Day (John 20:19–22). The Book of Acts says it was later, on the feast of Pentecost (Acts 2:1–4). The point is that awareness of the presence of the Spirit was primarily the experience of a gathering of believers in the Risen Lord, both initially and on later occasions (Acts 4:31; 10:44–48). That is why the Holy Spirit is the esprit de corps of the Church.

Theodore Wedel, a gifted twentieth-century theological teacher, used the analogy of school spirit. One has to be a member of the student body to know the spirit of a school; it is a part of the experience. A person who takes correspondence courses and never darkens the doors of the school will have no experience of that school's spirit. But when one does go forth from a school, having been a member of the student body, that school's spirit marks his life—for instance, he thinks and acts like a Harvard man.

In the New Testament members of the Church are called "saints" (1 Cor. 1:2). The Greek word for *saint* means "the holy ones"—they are members of the Holy Fellowship. There is a spiritual dimension, a beyond-this-world dimension which school spirit lacks. The members of the Church not only experience the Spirit's presence as they worship together, they live under the inspiration and guidance of the Holy Spirit or Holy Ghost (*ghost* is the old Anglo-Saxon word for "spirit"). They aspire to reflect "the fruit of the Spirit" in their lives—fruit which Paul describes as love, joy, peace, patience, kindness, goodness, faithfulness, gentleness, self-control (Gal. 5:22).

It is a practice in many churches to call upon the Holy Spirit to set apart for their holy purposes the water and the oil of chrism used in baptism, the bread and wine used in the Eucharist, the ring or rings used in marriage, and the persons ordained to the sacred ministry.

See Holy, God, Trinity.

Hope

HOPE for the Christian is the optimistic feeling that a person's faith in Jesus Christ gives him or her about the future.

Hope is bound up with being alive. The hopeless person is not likely to succeed; the hopeless sufferer is not likely to recover. Life and hope are intertwined: in the Bible, life and hope and faith in God are intertwined. Hope implies a looking forward to something good and favorable. This fundamental disposition is essential to the believer's life.

The Apostle Paul wisely beds down hope between faith and love (1 Cor. 13:13). They are natural bedfellows; we cannot separate hope from faith and love. The classic definition of faith is "the assurance of things hoped for" (Heb. 11:1), and it is our faith in the God of hope that fills us with joy and peace in believing (Rom. 15:13). So also with love. It is not possible to love one's neighbor without having hope for him. I pray for my sick friend because I love him and hope for his recovery. I give money to help feed the hungry because I care about them and hope that their condition will improve.

So faith, hope, and love describe a Christian at his deepest level. They depend on each other just as they also depend on the merciful goodness of God as known in Jesus Christ our Lord.

Christ the Lord is our living hope. The Christian's hope is not an idea but the living person of Jesus Christ, risen from the dead. By his Resurrection, Christ laid the foundation of hope in eternal life and delivers us from any crippling fear of what the future may bring.

Hope sets the Christian's life aglow and gives it zest.

I

Icon

AN ICON is a painting or image of a sacred personage—Christ, a saint, an angel—that is venerated as sacred. This practice is especially characteristic of the Eastern Orthodox church.

The set of mind of the Eastern churches differs from that of the Roman Catholic West. The tone of spirituality in the West was set in the sixth century by the founder of the Benedictine Order, Saint Benedict. His emphasis was on listening. The Byzantine fathers of the East focused on gazing.

Acting, speaking, and even reflective thinking are at times too demanding. There are times when one is too tired to pray or too distracted to read the Bible, but one can gaze. Seeing is something we do all the time. Even if we close our eyes we can see cars, people, trees, and colors, and when we sleep we dream in pictures. We do not have to be passive viewers. We can train ourselves to develop a spiritual life in the midst of our energy-draining society, through gazing. We can look at a picture meditatively, with the heart's eye, and let its deeper meaning of consolation and comfort flow over us.

This is the place of icons in the spiritual life of Eastern churches. Westerners may find icons rigid and lifeless, but to those who live with them and love them they have deep significance. As Henri J.M. Nouwen points out, "They speak more to our inner than to our outer senses. They speak to the heart that searches for God" (*Behold the Beauty of the Lord: Praying with Icons*, (1966) p. 14).

Christians in other traditions find this strange and foreign. However, many a person in the course of his or her devotions may regularly repeat the Lord's Prayer or a psalm or verses from the Bible or a hymn, and along with that act there occurs some mental picture—a stained glass window or a flower garden or one's mother laughing or cooking or praying, or some beautiful statue or picture. They see it in their mind's eye almost every time, and that vision becomes sacred for them.

Now you can begin to appreciate how for some a religious painting helps usher one into the presence of God.

Idolatry

IDOLATRY is the worship of a false god.

We immediately identify this practice with Hottentots and headhunters. But the practice of idol worship is insidious; it is as easy to become an idol worshiper without realizing it as it is to have high blood pressure without knowing it.

Idolatry is the practice of giving absolute "worth-ship" (worship) to someone or something that does not deserve it. In their proper place money, patriotism, moral principles, family loyalty, weight control, exercise, social prominence, "keeping up with the Joneses," and so on, have varying degrees of importance in our lives. However, none of them deserve to be the guiding principle of one's life. Many of us are idolaters without realizing it.

This applies as much to religiously inclined folk as to others. It is easy to give supreme worth to denomination or Bible, or liturgy or prayer book. It is easy to lose our sense of proportion. One of the Ten Commandments condemns idolatry:

> You shall not make for yourself any graven image, nor the likeness of anything that is in Heaven above, or that is in the earth beneath, or that is in the water under the earth; you shall not bow down to them, or worship them. (Exod. 20:4–5)

Most of us assume that this commandment is referring to tall totem poles or chubby sitting Buddhas and is not addressed to us. But rather, it is addressed to everyone for us, for it applies to all the possible things in our lives which we set up as standards by which life is to be judged. The Bible contains many warnings against this temptation. It is said that there is more written about the commandment against idol worship in the Old Testament than about all the other nine commandments combined, and with good reason.

See Worship.

Immortality of the Soul

THE IMMORTALITY OF THE SOUL is a term used by people who believe that although our bodies die and go "the way of all flesh," our souls survive and live forever. While this is a commonly held belief, it is not biblical. Christian thought stresses resurrection of the total person, body and soul. One's abandoned physical body will be replaced by "the body which is to be" (1 Cor. 15:37). God made us and loves us; after death we are raised (the whole of us, body and soul) by his power to newness of life with him. That is what the "resurrection of the body" in the Apostle's Creed is all about.

For many centuries Christians talked about the "immortality of the soul," but with a renewed emphasis on "biblical theology" the term immortality of the soul has become suspect for at least two reasons:

1. It fails to embrace the total person. Body and soul are inseparably one. My personality expresses itself through this particular body. I don't *have* a body; I *am* a body. Immortality of the soul separates me from my body; I wouldn't be all there without it; I wouldn't be *me*.

2. The concept considers the physical part of a person's life worthless and corrupt. The Bible says, Not so. God created all things—mountains and plants and fish and animals and human beings—everything. "And God saw everything that he had made, and behold, it was very good" (Gen. 1:31).

It is true that *immortality* is popularly used as a convenient synonym for *everlasting life*, or *life eternal*. But this practice should be recognized as shorthand for a grander and more satisfying biblical belief. For during our life on earth the loving Father of us all enables us to become sons and daughters fit for full fellowship with him, and he will continue and complete this relationship in his own time and in his own ways, beyond the confines of earthly life.

The idea of the immortality of the soul is based on the experience of man's indomitable spirit. The idea of the resurrection of the body is based on our faith of God's amazing love.

See Eternal Life, Incarnation, Resurrection of the Body.

Incarnation

INCARNATION is the distinctive Christian belief that in Jesus Christ God entered human life and became one of us. "The Word became flesh and dwelt among us, full of grace and truth" (John 1:14).

After reading a biography of President Franklin D. Roosevelt, a young man said, "I wish I had known him—*in the flesh.*" The word *incarnation* means exactly that: "being in the flesh."

"No one has ever seen God," writes John. "The only Son, who is in the bosom of the Father, he has made him known" (John 1:18). Jesus Christ was a fully human being, tempted in every way just as we are, but he was also the Son of God enabling us to see and know what God is like.

At first the disciples of Jesus saw him as a wonderful person and nothing more. The better they knew him, the more they felt a strange sense of awe. When he spoke of forgiveness, the forgiveness of God was unquestionably present. When he reached out to all kinds of distressed and afflicted persons, God's love and compassion came to life before their very eyes. When he died on the Cross, the disciples were shattered and disillusioned. But on the third day he rose from the dead. He was with them, saying familiar words, "Peace be with you," and doing familiar things like breaking bread with them. Thomas finally put their dawning conviction into words: "My Lord and my God."

A generation later Paul summed up this great Christian truth with: "He is the image of the invisible God" (Col. 1:15).

See Christ, Jesus.

"In Christ"

"IN CHRIST" is the way in which the Apostle Paul describes a Christian. "If anyone is in Christ he is a new creation" (2 Cor. 5:17) is his way of explaining the mystical experience in which one lives because Christ lives in him. We experience a somewhat similar change brought about because of an intimate friendship. Our outlook, our sense of what is important, and our standard of excellence seek to measure up to a new criteria so that we may be a worthy friend. We say, "We are simpatico." This mystical union is found in some degree in all intimate friendships, and need not be regarded as being beyond the experience of the ordinary person.

This relationship with Christ involves an even more profound inner change which is the equivalent of a "new creation." One is not improved, or reformed, or altered in any way that simply implies an external change, however great; he is remade. He is different even from what he was at his best. The change goes to the root of his being.

Here is Paul's description of the profound change a person undergoes: "I have been crucified with Christ; it is no longer I who live, but Christ who lives in me; and the life I now live in the flesh I live by faith in the Son of God, who loved me and gave himself for me" (Gal. 2:20).

Intercession

INTERCESSION is prayer for other people. It is telling God of your deep concern for somebody else, especially someone in special need, just as a daughter might bring the needs of her brothers and sisters to the attention of their father or mother.

Why should we think that our prayers should touch the lives of others? Paul writes about the Church as the Body of Christ, and calls us members or parts of that body. "If one member suffers, all suffer together; if one member is honored, all rejoice together" (1 Cor. 12:26). When you have a toothache, you may not hurt all over but you are certainly uncomfortable all over. So also in our corporate life. If there is a robbery in the neighborhood, all of us are more careful about locking our doors. If young people drive recklessly, everybody's car insurance premiums go up. We *are* members one of another. Our lives *are* interlaced with those of others.

These are analogies which help us come to grips with and appreciate intercessory prayer even though we cannot fully understand it.

Our Lord prayed for others. He said to Peter, "I have prayed for you that your faith fail not" (Luke 22:32). He prayed for children (Matt. 19:13). He urged his followers to "pray for those who persecute you" (Matt. 5:44). In John's Gospel we see Jesus as the Great Intercessor with the Father for all who are faithful to him (John 17:15).

When we pray for others, let us admit that there is mystery involved (*"Doesn't God know already? What good will my prayer do?"*). We don't know all the answers either about why praying for others is important or how it works. But we do know that when we pray earnestly, expectantly, persistently (remember Jesus' parable of the wicked judge and the persistent widow, Luke 18:1-7), something happens. Our prayer may be granted, causing us to sing with the psalmist, "This is the Lord's doing and it is marvelous in our eyes" (Ps. 118:23). Or things may not turn out the way we had hoped, but usually a change has taken place. For instance, a much-prayed-for grandmother may still have to cope with her arthritis, high blood pressure, and all the rest, but her attitude has changed.

Our prayers for others should have this twofold characteristic. On the one hand, they should be quite specific—pray for others by name and for their special needs as we lovingly perceive them. On the other hand, we should make our Lord's Gethsemane prayer our own—"nevertheless not my will, but thine be done" (Luke 22:42). Our Heavenly Father is infinitely more loving than we are, so we commend to his merciful concern those for whose needs we plead.

As intercessors we get up from our knees seeking ways in which we can help bring about the well-being of the persons for whom we have prayed. Thus we become willing agents of God's saving power.

See Petition, Prayer.

J

Jesus

JESUS is the name of the Son of God while he was a man on earth. It derives from the Hebrew name *Joshua* which means "God is help." The Jesus of the Gospels was known as "Jesus of Nazareth" for, although born in Bethlehem, he had been brought up in the city of Nazareth (Luke 4:16).

Following his baptism by John in the Jordan River and his temptations in the wilderness, Jesus returned to Galilee and began a ministry of teaching and healing (Luke 4:1–15), emphasizing the kingdom of God, the loving Father of all. Before long he was attracting large crowds and much attention (Mark 3:7–8).

From the numbers who followed him, Jesus selected twelve as his special disciples. They accompanied him wherever he went, and gradually it dawned on them that he was the long-awaited Messiah. His amazing authority over unclean spirits (Mark 1:27), over sickness (Luke 5:17–26), over the forces of nature (Mark 4:41), and his ability to forgive sin (Luke 5:18–26) and even raise the dead (Mark 5:35–48) convinced them that he was truly Lord of all.

The strict Pharisees and other religious leaders found Jesus' teaching unacceptable (Mark 2:23–3:6). The ultimate encounter with the authorities came when Jesus went to Jerusalem at Passover time. Through the treachery of Judas, one of the disciples, Jesus was arrested by stealth, tried in a sham trial, and crucified. Three days later his closest friends and disciples experienced his risen presence.

The Resurrection appearances make it quite clear that the Risen Lord is the same person who walked the roads of Galilee.

Christ, the Greek word for "messiah," became associated with his name as a title after the Resurrection. In time Christ ceased to be used as a title, Jesus who is the Christ, and was used as part of his name: Jesus Christ.

See Christ, God, Kingdom of God, Trinity.

Justification

JUSTIFICATION is the merciful gift of God's bringing us into a healthy relationship with himself, even though we are unworthy sinners. To *justify* means "to free from guilt"; as the word occurs in the New Testament it can well be translated, "put in the right with God." It is a metaphor drawn from the law courts, one of the many metaphors which describe Christian salvation. Our justification involves trusting in God's righteousness and mercy as we have come to know it in Jesus Christ. This is the central theme of the gospel of salvation.

All of us yearn for acceptance, recognition, esteem, and respect. We seek to fulfill this yearning by our own efforts and ingenuity. But Jesus makes it clear that this will not work. He once told a parable about two men worshiping in the temple. One was a Pharisee and his prayer (bragging, really) was telling God all the commendable things he had done, while in the process looking down on his fellow worshipers. He felt certain God would be impressed; certainly, he thought, his behavior had earned him God's favor. The other man was a despised tax collector, a sinner by all standards of Jewish society. He simply prayed, "God, be merciful to me, a sinner." Jesus' comment was that "this man went down to his house, justified rather than the other" (Luke 18:9–14).

In thinking about what Jesus said, Paul (and later Martin Luther) concludes that everyone comes into a right relationship with God through trusting in God's mercy (*his* righteousness), not through doing good and pious things. Faith means being open to receive God's mercy as shown forth in Christ. And the characteristic of one who is living by faith in God's mercy is a stream of good works done out of gratitude.

We are on the wrong track when we attempt to justify ourselves in God's eyes by our good works. That always fails. Apart from faith in God's merciful goodness our good works turn out to be an exercise in *self*-justification. We look upon our good works with pride, and this separates us from others. That is what happened to the Pharisee in Jesus' parable.

The basic truth is that the acceptance we yearn for cannot be bought. We cannot buy friendship and esteem from other human beings or from God. Acceptance and love are always gifts. The wonderful truth about our relationship with God becomes clear in Jesus

Christ: "God shows his love for us in that while we were yet sinners Christ died for us" (Rom. 5:8). Faith is trust in this good news, acceptance of the fact that we are accepted.

The result of all this is that we can forget about the problem of our salvation because it has been accomplished for us. Our only concern now is to express our thanksgiving to God for his gracious gift by loving our neighbors, and by imitating God in accepting those who are unacceptable.

See Atonement, Faith, Reconciliation, Salvation, Sin.

K

Kingdom of God

THE KINGDOM OF GOD and the Reign of God are terms referring to God's rule through Christ. At the time Jesus lived, a king was in complete control of his subjects. A good king was like a shepherd; he cared about his people and looked after them. A king is not elected, nor do we elect God king. God is *always* King. It is sensible and right that he should rule because he created everything and knows how things should work. We have only to accept his rule and things will be as he planned them. Nothing that works against God's rule can last.

God's people, the Jews, always dreamed of a time when his rule would be universal. At first they thought this would happen through a king of Israel. When things went badly for them and their kings were defeated, they looked for a king from heaven. He would be sent by God and would be anointed by him as a king was anointed. So they called him "Messiah," which means "the anointed one."

Then Jesus came. He said, "The time is fulfilled, the kingdom of God is at hand; repent, and believe the gospel (Mark 1:15). Wherever he went wonderful things happened. The sick were healed, lepers were cleansed, demons were cast out. His teaching had an authority that amazed people. Where Jesus was, the power and love of god were at work in a new way.

In one sense, the Kingdom of God was already present in the person of Jesus. Everything he said and did made the rule of God a present reality for those close to him. On the other hand, Jesus taught his disciples to pray, "Thy kingdom come, thy will be done." Somewhere in the future the time would come when God's kingly rule would be recognized and he would be accepted as Sovereign overall.

We experience something of the kingdom in the life of the Church, where Christ is worshiped and his ways are accepted; it is in a small way a preview of what the kingdom will finally be like. However, our human capacity for messing things up infects even our religious behavior, and we must acknowledge that the Lord will establish his kingdom fully in his own good time, quite apart from our human efforts or the unfolding of history.

Matthew's Gospel uses "Kingdom of Heaven" rather than Kingdom of God which reflects the Jewish reticence to pronounce the Name of God. Out of reverence "Heaven" is used as a substitute.

See Christ, Eschatology.

L

Lectionary

THE LECTIONARY is a list of appointed Scripture readings (lections) for public worship on the Sundays and holy days of the church year. In recent years the lectionary has become an element of unity among American churches.

This began with the publication of the Roman Catholic *Ordo Lectionum Missae* in 1969. During the following decade variations of that Roman lectionary came into use in a number of American churches. The Presbyterian *Worshipbook* (1970) and the Episcopalian *Book of Common Prayer* (1979) base their lectionaries on it, as does *The Church Year—Calendar and Lectionary* (1973) of the Inter-Lutheran Commission on Worship. Variations of it have been adopted by the United Church of Christ, the Christian church (Disciples of Christ) and the Methodist church. So in a few short years an amazing number of churches in the United States and Canada have begun using lectionaries which are more notable for their similarities than for their differences.

The characteristics of these lectionaries are that for each Sunday there are three appointed Scripture readings—Old Testament, Epistle, and Gospel—plus an appropriate psalm or portion thereof. The lectionary is laid out in a three-year cycle. In Year A (which always begins with Advent in years divisible by three) Matthew's Gospel is read almost in its entirety. In Year B Mark is read; and in Year C, Luke. Portions of the Fourth Gospel are read in all three years on the great feasts, during Lent and Holy Week, and in the Easter season. The basic pattern is generally the same. The same Gospel passage with variations is almost invariably read. Denominational variations have usually been in the appointed Old Testament or Epistle readings.

The visible unity of the Church of our Lord may be for Church representatives around the conference table a distant objective. But for rank and file worshipers in the pews the oneness of the Church is being experienced as they hear the same portions of Scripture read and explained Sunday after Sunday.

See Church Year, Ecumenical.

Liturgy

LITURGY is the public worship of the Church shared in by both minister and people. A liturgical service has a plan and an order, although there may be provision for spontaneity. The people as well as the minister who leads the service have a definite part to play, and it cannot properly be held unless both the leader and the people take their respective parts. It is because those who assemble have in common a responsibility to participate that the prayer book of the Episcopal church is entitled "The Book of *Common* Prayer." Liturgical services are not a spectator sport, there is no audience. People have congregated together to worship God—a congregation.

"The Liturgy" is also one of the names of the Lord's Supper, the Mass, or the Holy Communion. In the Eastern Church that sacrament is known as the "Divine Liturgy."

Lord

LORD is usually thought of in Christian circles as a title for Jesus Christ. A lord is a master or ruler. As a title, "My lord" is the way in which a nobleman is addressed; the title carries with it the sense of superiority and authority.

Here are some of the circumstances in which Jesus' disciples became aware of his lordship.

- They saw him as Lord over the forces of nature when he calmed the storm on the lake. "They were filled with awe, and said to one another, 'Who then is this, that even wind and sea obey him?'" (Mark 4:41).
- Those present in the synagogue saw Jesus as Lord over evil spirits when he healed a man so afflicted. "With authority he commands even unclean spirits and they obey him" (Mark 1:27), they said in amazement.
- When a paralyzed man was lowered into his presence through a hole in the roof, Jesus both healed him and forgave his sins (Luke 5:17–26). Those present realized that this man Jesus was Lord over sin as well as sickness.

- When he turned Zacchaeus' whole life around, people recognized that he was Lord over the hearts of men and women (Luke 19:1-10).
- And when he raised to life the daughter of the ruler of the synagogue, he was recognized to be Lord over death (Mark 5:21-43).

At every turn Jesus' power and authority overcame the evil forces which drag people down and enslave them.

When the forces of evil conspired to bring about his death on the Cross, God raised him from the dead. Here then was the capstone on his lordship. He is unquestionably Lord over both sin and death. As John the Seer put it years later: "He is Lord of lords and King of kings" (Rev. 17:14).

In looking back on who Jesus was and what he had done, Paul hymned his praise with, "At the name of Jesus every knee should bow, in heaven and on earth, and every tongue confess that Jesus Christ is Lord, to the glory of God the Father" (Phil. 2:10-11).

The earliest Christian creed was the basic declaration, "Jesus is Lord."

So it was only natural that the disciples and Christian believers from that day to this have recognized him as Lord, praised him as Lord, and vested their faith in Jesus Christ the Lord.

Love

TO LOVE means to care very deeply. But the word is used for a spectrum of meanings as far apart as the sublime attitude of God in Christ who died for us to the most sordid violations of the prohibition of adultery in the Ten Commandments. All of us want to love and be loved, and this built-in human longing expresses itself in a variety of ways. There is the romantic love of boy and girl, the tender love of mother and baby, the heroic love between comrades on the battlefield. There is also the adoring love we have for God, and the amazing, gracious love of God for us.

God made us and looked upon his creation as good. He also gave us his commandments—"the way in which we should go." But we humans rebelled against him, managing our affairs in defiance of him and to our detriment; we were sinners. In the Bible God both condemns human unfaithfulness and yearns over his people:

> When Israel was a child, I loved him . . .
> (yet) My people are bent on turning from me . . .
> How can I give you up, O Ephraim! . . .
> I will not execute my fierce anger . . .
> and I will not come to destroy. (Hos. 11:1, 9)

God shows his love for us by giving his only Son so that whoever believes in him will not perish but have everlasting life (John 3:16). Moreover, Christ showed his love for us by his self-giving life and death, and the New Testament writers are awed by the wonder of it. "By this we know love [in Greek, *agape*] that he laid down his life for us!" (1 John 3:16; see also Rom. 5:8).

Also this divine love which caused Christ to become one with us is a "binding tie" (Col. 3:14) that makes us one body in Christ (Rom. 12:5). Thus the Christian church springs from the agape of God. And the fruit of being a member of that company of believers is in striving to practice that same self-giving, serving, helping love. The Parable of the Good Samaritan (Luke 10:25–37) provides an illustration of what this means.

The sum of the matter is that "We love, because he first loved us" (1 John 4:19).

See Forgiveness.

M

Matrimony

HOLY MATRIMONY is a solemn and public covenant between a man and a woman sealed in the presence of God. In the course of this rite they legally become husband and wife and receive God's blessing as they begin life together.

The service takes place in the presence of a congregation or of at least two witnesses, and the marriage must conform to the laws of the state as well as the canons of the Church. It is intended to be a lifelong union which in the New Testament is compared to the relation of Christ and the Church (Eph. 5:23). That comparison underscores the solemn, unbreakable character of the marriage vows. Those vows in the services of the Episcopal and Methodist churches are spelled out more realistically than they are in some other churches. The bride and groom are promising to share each other's life no matter what circumstances arrive: "for better for worse, for richer for poorer, in sickness and in health, to love and to cherish, until we are parted by death."

Sometimes a couple who have been legally married by a civil authority wish to have the Church's blessing on their marriage. Both the Presbyterian *Worshipbook* and the Episcopalian *Book of Common Prayer* provide services for such an occasion.

Mediator

A MEDIATOR is a reconciler who brings estranged persons together. We are familiar with that role in an industrial strike: the mediator brings management and labor union officials together and works out an agreement.

The idea of a person being a mediator between God and humankind is found throughout the Bible. The mediator in the Old Testament is always an historical figure, a person who serves under the authority of God. (The term "mediator" is applied to an angel in Job 33:23, but the context indicates that he is only an intercessor.)

Moses' role at the time of the golden calf incident in the wilderness dramatically illustrates the work of a true mediator in Exodus, chapter 32. He first intercedes with God on behalf of the idol-worshipping Israelites (Exod. 32:7-14). Then in turn he seeks to bring them back into a faithful relationship with God (Exod. 32:30-32). He speaks the Word of God; he suffers for his people; he intercedes for them; he takes his place both with his people and "before God." The prophets also fill this role, and we see it profoundly illustrated by the Suffering Servant of God, in Isaiah 52:13-53:12.

In these same ways Jesus is the Mediator. He carries on his work for his people with the humility and obedience which leads to the Cross. He suffers for sin, enduring for us the effects of our sin. Thus, "he is the mediator of a New Covenant" with God through his blood. Because of the work of Christ the Mediator "those who are called receive the promised eternal inheritance" (Heb. 9:15). In John's Gospel, Christ is the mediator-intercessor; he prays for those whom God "has given him" (John 17:1-26), feeds them, guides them, gives himself for them.

Human sin has kept God and humankind apart. God takes the initiative. He sends his Son to bring men and women back to him. As a second generation churchman sums up the matter, "There is one God, and there is one mediator between God and men, the man Christ Jesus" (1 Tim. 2:5). This is one way our early Christian forebears sought to help us understand Jesus Christ. We come to the Father in prayer through him who calls us friends, our Mediator. And, in turn, the Father speaks to us through this same Mediator, his Son.

To refer to Christ as Mediator and of him as reconciling the world to himself are slightly different ways of describing the same aspect of Christian Good News.

See Intercession, Reconciliation, Suffering Servant.

Ministry

THE MINISTRY designates the responsibilities of every Christian, lay-persons as well as clergy. By virtue of his or her baptism every Christian has entered upon such a ministry.

Every baptized person's occupation in shop or field, in office or school or home is his or her "church work." That is the place where he or she carries on a witness to the saving power of God in Christ; Paul called it a "ministry of reconciliation" (2 Cor. 5:18). In addition, many laypersons assist in the worship and governance of the Church. They carry on this second kind of church work as lay-readers, choir members, acolytes, ushers, Sunday school teachers, church board or vestry members and in a host of other significant roles that make the Church's worship and witness more effective.

The Lord's Great Commission to carry the Good News of God in Christ to the people of the world, whether in distant places or destitute neighborhoods, is carried on primarily by laypersons. Doctors and teachers and social workers and anthropologists, Peace Corps workers abroad and VISTA workers at home, all might be called the tip of the iceberg. Hosts of other people, who do not even think of themselves as "missionaries," in the way that they live in the course of their daily pursuits bear witness to the saving power of God. Paul describes this ministry as "ambassadors for Christ, God making his appeal through us" (2 Cor. 5:20).

Such is the ministry of laypersons. The ordained ministry is described elsewhere in this book.

See Order of Ministers.

Miracle

A MIRACLE is a happening in the natural world which defies any normal explanation and is considered the work of God. The times described in the Bible are full of miracles. Is today different? Perhaps. Perhaps not.

God is still as much at work in his world today as he ever has been. We are not aware of this fact, probably because we, like Woody Allen, expect God to be an underachiever. There is a biblical story of the widow of Zarephath who because of the drought had exhausted her supply of food and money and was certain she and her son would soon starve to death. Then the Prophet Elijah came to stay with them and her food supply miraculously did not run out (1 Kings 17:8–16). There is the story of another widow, this one living near Washington, D.C. She was laid off from her job, her unemployment insurance had come to an end, and she was walking the street half praying, half crying, desperate. A lady walked up to her and said, "Do you know where I can get somebody to work for me? I have a big house. I need to have my house cleaned and I need a cook." Those two women were both happy and one of them still had tears in her eyes . . . tears of thanksgiving. In the Bible such a happening was called a miracle.

An ill friend sought the prayers of his church for his recovery. On the day before his operation his diagnosed cancer somehow disappeared. Coincidence? Just lucky? Or was his experience a modern version of Jesus' healing of the paralytic (Mark 2:1–12)? His doctors reacted with the same wonder as did the people in the synagogue with Jesus when he healed the man. And they said exactly the same thing: "We never saw anything like this before!"

Miracles do happen today. Lots of them. All around us. Only those who have the eyes of faith recognize them for what they are.

Mission

THE MISSION of the Church is to carry the Good News of Jesus Christ to everyone everywhere. Jesus said, "As the Father has sent me, even so I send you" (John 20:21). Jesus himself was God's great missionary to humankind, and every baptized Christian has promised to continue his work. The Church has a worldwide mission: "Go into all the world and make disciples" is our Lord's command.

Every person in the world needs to know that he or she belongs to God and that God cares about, loves, forgives, and sustains each person. One of the ways the Church shows people God's love for them is to put church buildings, ministers, teachers, hospitals, and schools wherever they are needed. The worldwide mission of the Church is never finished.

The first thing the American pioneers did when they climbed down from their covered wagons was to start a church. They were missionaries, perhaps, without realizing it. At one time missionaries brought the Good News of Jesus Christ to your town and started churches there. Thanks to them you have churches in which to pray, to hear the gospel, and to receive the sacraments.

We are thankful that God so loved the world that he sent his Son, Jesus Christ, the Great Missionary. We are thankful for the missionaries who brought the Good News of God in Christ to the place where we live. This gratitude of ours for God's love and forgiveness and sustaining power which comes to us through Jesus Christ needs to find expression in our lives—in what we say and do, in our treatment of others, in our attitude toward life and the world God has given us. This thankful living is our Christian witness.

Each of us shares in carrying out the mission of the Church on two levels—that which we do firsthand, the influence of our lives on the world around us, and that which we help to happen in distant places.

Your firsthand share in the mission of the Church is in the circle of influence where you spend your working day—office, school, hospital, factory, shop. Wherever you earn your living, wherever you live your days, is the place where you can advance the mission of the Church.

We enter the other and wider sphere of that mission through our giving. The monetary contribution you make to your church is used in part to further the mission of the Church in distant places.

See Alms/Offering, Ministry.

Mystery

THE MYSTERY of the Christian faith is that which we do not understand and, try as we might, cannot fully understand. Mystery in the New Testament refers to the revelation in Jesus Christ and in the Church of the grand redemptive plan of God.

Mystery is a New Testament word. There is no exact equivalent of the term *mystery* in Hebrew. When the early Church came in contact with the Greek world, Paul first and then others adopted that Greek word to help interpret the Christian faith to Gentile believers.

Some mysteries, like murder-mystery stories, must be solved in order that the truth be known. But other mysteries become even more profound as we learn more about them. The mysteries of God, of Jesus Christ, of the Christian church fall into this latter class. Here is a list of the bafflements which form the crux of the Christian faith:

- At the same time that Jesus Christ comes and reveals himself, he is hidden.
- God has chosen the weak things of the world to confound the strong.
- In order to reveal eternity, he has chosen time.
- In order to reveal his Spirit, he has chosen flesh.
- In order to reveal his divinity, he has chosen a human being.
- In order to cause his sovereignty to shine forth, he has chosen the Cross.
- To reveal his presence to the ages, he has chosen our lives and those of our forebears.
- To make his voice sound forth he uses the stammerings of his servants.
- To unite all people in one Body he has chosen the fallible Christian church.
- He uses the catastrophes of the history of nations to lead us on the way to the new Jerusalem.

You and I would have thought it more appropriate to do these things in some other way. We wonder why God did it all as he did. Mystery!

It is no wonder that in preaching "to the Gentiles the unsearchable riches of Christ" the author of Ephesians says that his goal is "to make all men see what is the plan of the mystery hidden for ages in God who created all things" (Eph. 3:9).

And you and I experience a part of the mystery of God's plan every time we come to the Lord's Table to receive the Sacrament of bread and wine. How do a bit of bread and a few drops of wine become the vehicles of the Lord strengthening grace whereby Christ enters our lives and sustains us? Mystery. Paul agrees; listen to him: "How great among the Gentiles are the riches of the glory of this mystery, which is Christ in you, the hope of glory" (Col. 2:27). It is no wonder that the Sacrament of bread and wine are sometimes called "these holy mysteries."

N

Name

YOUR NAME is the term by which you are known. Traditionally, when a person becomes a member of the "household of God" in Holy Baptism, that person is given his or her Christian name— Charles, Sarah, Virginia, Joseph. A person's last name (surname) traditionally was the *Yellow Pages* part of their identity; a person was called "Baker" because that is what they did and they lived on Baker Street. But your Christian name is a distinctive part of you, received when you were "christened," when you became a Christian. In the baptismal service the Name of God, Father, Son, and Holy Spirit was linked with yours, signifying the covenant agreement between you and God which is the basic significance of baptism.

If you have ever been in a strange city and had someone on the street or in the airport call you by name—a chance meeting with a friend—you have discovered something special about your name. When that person called your name, "all the king's horses and all the king's men" could not have kept you from turning around to find out who it was. To pronounce a person's name is to have a certain power over him. Because of this fact, the Old Testament Jews did not pronounce the Name of God; they used some term that stood for God, such as the Most High or the Lord. Why? Reverence. One does not presume to have power over God. We see it also in Matthew's Gospel—he speaks of the "Kingdom of *Heaven*," never the "Kingdom of God." God's Name is, therefore, so sacred that we do not use it lightly or casually or unthinkingly—"vainly," says one of the Ten Commandments.

Your Christian name is important to you, too. It is generally used in Church in special prayers when you are sick, when you are married, and other important times. In a deep sense your name represents *you*. You endorse a friend's check which means that you will make his check good if he does not have enough money in the bank; your name on his check means that your integrity stands behind him.

We pray in the Name of Jesus Christ, meaning according to his Spirit—that is, we have tried to pray the kind of prayer on which he would put his initials, his approval. We do not use his Name carelessly, just as we would not want anyone to use our names as though we endorse something of which we do not approve.

See Baptism, Covenant.

Neighbor

YOUR NEIGHBOR is the person who needs you. That was Jesus' unexpected definition when a lawyer asked him for one. Except that Jesus did not go around giving legal definitions of what one should or should not do; he told stories—parables—to picture the situation and left it to his hearers to frame their own definitions. The Parable of the Good Samaritan (Luke 10:25–37) is a good example.

Legal definitions are like fences: they shut people out. "My neighbor is person who lives on my block or goes to my church or is white or is Protestant or is a Gentile or respectfully asks for help." To these and all the many unspoken fences of limitation on whom I will help and whom not, Jesus would probably say, "Horsefeathers!" (Remember he was truly a man so he got impatient with human littleness and pettiness just like you and I do.) And then, maybe he'd add a re-run of the Good Samaritan and rephrase the punch line: "Your neighbor is anyone, ANYone who needs your help." No legal fences.

The parable describes the Samaritan as giving the man in the ditch all-out help—he gave him first aid, a ride to the inn, nursing care, and promise of a follow-up payment. He gave him everything he himself would have wanted to receive had he been in the victim's situation. If you want a rule, there it is. Do everything for your neighbor that you would want to have done for you were you in the same situation. That is the golden rule of neighborliness.

O

Order of Ministers

ORDER OF MINISTERS refers to the ranks of ordained clergy.

Historically, a bishop is the chief pastor of the Church. The bishop is responsible for the Church in a geographic area called a diocese. The word *bishop* literally means "overseer"; the Greek word is *episkopos*, from which *episcopal* is derived. In the Eastern Orthodox church a bishop is often called a "metropolitan." This is probably the case because the first bishops were overseers of churches in and around some city. The bishop is not only the overseer of the clergy and people of the diocese but also the guardian of the faith, worship, and life of the church in that jurisdiction. This authority the bishop received from his or her predecessors and will pass on to his or her successors. The bishop represents the whole Church.

A bishop is the chief shepherd and the spiritual leader of all the people of a diocese, with responsibility and authority to carry on the apostles' teaching and to continue the fellowship of the Church. Both what is preached and taught, and the mode of worship is under the bishop's authority.

In some dioceses there are assistant bishops. An assistant may be a bishop coadjutor—one who will automatically become head of the diocese when the bishop dies or retires, or a suffragan bishop—one who remains an assistant until he is elected bishop or bishop coadjutor.

The Episcopal church follows this historic pattern of the bishop being the chief shepherd and spiritual leader of the people of a diocese. There are a number of variations of this form of polity. In the Lutheran churches the geographic area is called a district and is headed by a president, sometimes called a bishop. A group of churches within a certain geographic area in the Methodist church is called a district which is presided over by a superintendent; a group of districts form a conference which is headed by a bishop. A group of churches in the Presbyterian church form a presbytery presided over by an executive officer and a moderator.

Presbyter and *priest* and *elder* are interrelated terms all stemming from the same Greek word. All of them designate the clergyperson in charge of a congregation.

In the Methodist Church the elder is the minister in charge of a congregation. In the Episcopal church he or she is a priest. In the Lutheran, Presbyterian, and Roman Catholic churches that person is called the pastor. In all of these churches he or she is frequently referred to as the minister.

In the Methodist and Episcopal Churches there is a junior rank of ordained ministers called a *deacon*. The Presbyterian church uses the titles "deacon" and "elder" in another way.

Custom as well as officialdom has bestowed a variety of titles on the local clergyperson, usually indicating some aspect of his or her responsibility. A preacher is, obviously, one who preaches. A minister is a person who ministers to or serves his or her people. A pastor is the shepherd of the flock, caring for them, attending to their spiritual needs. Father is the title of a person who is head of the family of God's people. Rector is the head of an Episcopal parish; he directs the work of that local church. A parson is the chief person in a congregation, its spiritual leader. It is only proper to call a clergyperson doctor if he or she holds a doctor's degree.

See Apostolic Succession, Ministry, Ordination.

Ordination

ORDINATION means to invest a person with some ecclesiastical authority. It usually means to confer holy orders or ministerial orders on a person which is to vest him or her with the authority to exercise the office of one of the ordained ministries. This is the normal pattern in Lutheran, Episcopal, Roman, and Eastern Orthodox churches. In the Presbyterian church, however, laypersons are ordained to offices of deacon and elder with responsibilities within their congregation for a stated term.

See Order of Ministers.

Outreach

OUTREACH is a term used to describe the Church's missionary concern. There was a day when the Church thought in terms of "home missions" and "foreign missions," geographic designations. But missionary concern is better described as concern to reach out beyond the immediate operation and functioning of the Church – whether that be the local congregation, the diocese, the district, or the national Church – to minister to those who are outside that circle. To suburbanites, church outreach may include finding a way to express their concern for those who live in the inner city ghetto or on a prison farm. To a diocese or district it may include not only support of their church nationally but also close ties with some church or churches in another land. And your church may involve itself in a ministry to migrant farm workers, or to college work, or to a cooperative ministry with other denominations in some Third World country. Outreach is an effort to find a way to respond to the command, "Go ye into all the world."

See Mission.

P–Q

Parable

A PARABLE is a story or a description of something familiar from which a moral or spiritual truth is drawn. In its pure form it has a single lesson to convey. Jesus' Parable of the Unscrupulous Judge and the Widow (Luke 18:1–7) is a case in point. In it Jesus is teaching that sincere persistence is one of the attributes of genuine prayer.

All of Jesus' teaching stories are called parables. However, some of them have come down to us in the revised form which resulted from their retelling and use in the early Church. The Parable of the Sower and the Seed (Mark 4:3–20) is an example. Jesus' original parable was probably only verses three through eight. He was encouraging his disciples to believe that the preaching of the Kingdom would prove fruitful. However, in use the emphasis shifted and it became a parable of the soils, each soil receiving the seed differently (Mark 4:10–20). In use the parable had become an allegory, each detail having its own significance. What had been a parable of encouragement has now become an allegory of warning.

Passover

THE PASSOVER is the great Jewish feast celebrating the deliverance of the Israelites from Egyptian bondage.

Biblical accounts of the deliverance recount several plagues that smote Egypt due to the Pharaoh's repeated refusal to let the Israelites go. During the final plague, God sent an angel of death to slay the firstborn son in every household. To avoid this tragedy themselves, the Israelites were instructed in advance to slay a lamb, and to smear the lamb's blood on the doorposts of their houses. The lamb itself was to be roasted and eaten at one final, hasty meal, while the Israelites stood prepared to travel.

The Israelites were told:

> For the Lord will pass through to slay the Egyptians, and when he sees the blood on the lentel and on the two doorposts, the Lord will *pass*

over [emphasis mine] the door, and will not allow the destroyer to enter your houses to slay you. You shall observe this rite as an ordinance for you and for your sons forever. (Exod. 12:23-24)

So it was that the Israelites were saved by the blood of a lamb.

The Passover is observed for seven days following the full moon at the end of March or early in April. The details regarding this feast are found in Exodus 12:1-20.

The Peace

THE PEACE or THE KISS OF PEACE was an early Christian greeting. Today, "The Peace" is the title of a portion of the liturgy when people exchange the greeting, "The Peace of the Lord be always with you," and the response, "And also with you." A handshake often accompanies this exchange. Paul repeatedly concludes his epistles with, "Greet all the brethren with a holy kiss" (Rom. 16:16; 1 Cor. 16:20; 2 Cor. 13:12; 1 Thess. 5:16). The practice became a regular part of the celebration of the Lord's Supper down through the centuries. At the time of the Reformation the words, "The peace of the Lord be always with you" were a part of the Episcopal service in the first *Book of Common Prayer* published in 1549, but the Episcopalians omitted it for a time. The Lutherans and Presbyterians subsequently omitted the practice, and two hundred years later, so did the Methodists. The Presbyterians made "The Peace" a regular part of their worship again in 1972 as did the Lutherans in 1978 and the Episcopalians in 1979. About the time of the Second Vatican Council (1970) "The Peace" which had always been part of the Mass as a verbal response became a ceremonial greeting between members of the congregation as well as the clergy.

From at least the fifth century "The Peace" has most often taken place in the service immediately following the intercessions. It was considered something of a dramatic way to put the stamp of corporate concern on the petitions just offered. The appropriateness of placing "The Peace" after the prayers and just before the offertory probably goes back to the injunction in the Sermon on the Mount, "First be reconciled to your brother and then come and offer your gift" (Matt. 5:24). The greeting, "The Peace of the Lord be with you," may antedate the kiss itself. In the Risen Lord's initial appearance to the gathered disciples his first words were, "Peace be with you." "Then the disciples were glad when they saw the Lord" (John 20:19, 20). This greeting was a part of his identity as being the same person with whom they had walked the roads of Galilee; it was so characteristic of him. It would have been a natural thing when they gathered in his Name to greet one another as he had greeted them. So not only was the Supper of the Lord celebrated in remembrance of him, probably the Lord's characteristic greeting was also done in that service in remembrance of him.

Penitence

PENITENCE is turning to God in sorrow after we have done something wrong. Penitence and repentance and contrition are words with intertwined meanings. They are almost like different facets of the same gem; when we look at it from a different angle the highlights are different but it is the same stone. The Prodigal Son (Luke 15:11–32) was penitent: he was very sorry for what he had done. He was repentant: he turned about and changed his way of life. When he returned home he was contrite: he expressed his sorrow for having offended his father.

Look more closely at the words penitence and repentance: both concern sorrow for sin, for having done something wrong. But they are not exactly the same. Penitence means "I am very sorry." To be truly sorry I don't have to be all stirred up inside, but I have to admit my fault and resolve to change my ways. Repentance refers more to the things I do because I am sorry. For instance, I turn to God, I confess my sins, I pray that the injury I have done to another person may be healed, and I determine to help to heal it. I promise myself, and God, that I will try to do better. Repentance is a turning around in attitude and action.

If you start to smoke, having promised your family not to, and get caught, you may be sorry about it. If your feelings are sincere, you are a penitent. Whether or not you are repentant will depend upon what you do about it. When you admit your transgression and promise not to do it again, you are beginning to "turn about." This action is necessary for penitence to become repentance. Just to be sorry that you got caught is not enough; you may simply try to

find a more secret place to smoke next time. In that case you are neither penitent nor repentant.

Now about contrition: If you realize that something you have
said or done has hurt your best friend, you are likely to be contrite.
Because your friend loves you and trusts you, you are very sorry
you have offended him or her; you hate yourself for what you have
done. A similar guilt, remorse, and deep desire to make amends
arises in us when we think of how we have sinned and yet how very
much God loves us. He sent his Son into the world to live and die
for people like me! This is when we realize how much it must hurt
the loving Heavenly Father when we are selfish and little and mean.

Read these penitential psalms: 32, 51, 130; then read Psalm 103.
They help you see that once you have acknowledged your sin, God
forgives you. You also see that all these psalms end in an act of
praise and thanksgiving for forgiveness.

See Confession, Forgiveness.

Petition

PETITION is prayer for ourselves. We are meant to turn to God with
our own needs just as we turn to him with the needs of others.
Indeed, all that is said about intercessory prayer is applicable to our
prayers for ourselves. One is an extension of the other.

While we may be quite specific about that for which we pray—a
better job, more money, help to get out of a difficulty, and so on—we
also ask him to help us as *he* sees fit. Our Lord's Garden of Gethsemane prayer becomes our own—"Not my will, but thine be done"
(Luke 22:42). For Jesus this meant the Cross. The all-wise and loving Father of us all may not grant our petition as such, but may help
us to accept rather than avoid suffering. Then he provides the
strength we need to cope.

Both petition and intercession make us aware of God's power at
work in our lives and in the lives of others. Because we take our con-
cerns to God with earnest persistence our eyes are opened to how
very often wonderful things happen. William Temple once warned,
"When you stop praying, coincidences stop."

See Intercession, Prayer.

Pharisees

THE PHARISEES were the strict law-abiding sect in Jewish society and were people of great religious zeal. They were laymen and scholars, not priests, uncompromising in their observance of religious ceremonies and practices and in adherence to oral laws and traditions. As a consequence of their zeal they had expanded the Ten Commandments into seven hundred-plus regulations, all of which they believed should be observed. In contrast to the Sadducees, the other major sect in Jewish society, the Pharisees followed a liberal interpretation of the Law of God. The Sadducees did not recognize the authority of religious practices and laws not found in the Pentateuch (the first five books of the Old Testament).

In the Gospels "Pharisees and scribes" are usually mentioned together. The scribes were the scholars among the Pharisees who copied the contents of the scrolls of Scripture, which was the only way additional copies could be produced. Because the scribes copied the Law they knew the Law and were authorities on the subject. In the Gospels they are sometimes called "lawyers" (Luke 10:25).

See Commandments, Sadducees.

Piety

PIETY is reverence toward God and shows itself in the devout fulfillment of religious obligations. There is a strong undertone of loyalty. The psalmist speaks of those pious Jews who out of loyalty to God oppose every compromise with the pagan religion of their neighbors. They are called the godly (Ps. 4:3) and the saints (Ps. 85:8-9). The intense spiritual life of the pious springs not only from love and prayer but also from "acts of piety"—vows (Ps. 76:11), sacrifices (2 Chron. 29:31), offerings and alms (Neh. 13:13-14), and fasting (Dan. 10:2-3).

In the New Testament there is much teaching about piety in the Gospels (Matt. 6:1-18; Luke 18:1-14, etc.) and in the Epistles (Rom. 12; 2 Cor. 8-9; Phil. 4, etc.) but, strangely the word does not appear.

The pious are those who have a sense of duty in expressing their reverence toward God and their consequent behavior toward others. The pervading temptation of pious folks is always to look down on those who do not share their dedicated zeal. Jesus often spoke out against the hypocrisy (Luke 12:1), the self-righteousness (Luke 18:9–14), and the coldheartedness (Mark 3:1–6) of the religious leaders of his people. One's acts of reverence and devotion must be coupled with humility to be acceptable to God (Matt. 5:5, 8; Luke 18:13–14). And at the same time, godliness and moral virtues—such as integrity (1 Tim. 2:2) and right dealings (1 Tim. 6:11)—cannot be separated (John 4:21).

True piety, then, is sincere, steadfast, and completely humble. It is of piety that the claim is made: "Godliness is of value in every way, as it holds promise for the present life and for the life to come" (1 Tim. 4:8).

Praise

PRAISE is a joyful form of prayer which is usually set to music. Somewhere between adoration and thanksgiving, praise raises its voice. But unlike adoration and thanksgiving, praise almost has to sing or shout its feeling in the presence of God.

A *doxology* is a hymn of praise to God. The best known doxology is "Praise God from whom all blessings flow." It, of course, can be said, but it is highly combustible material: it is likely to burst into song. The same is also true of "Alleluia," a variation of *Hallelujah*, the Hebrew exclamation which means "Praise the Lord."

Hosanna is a shout of praise and adoration to God. The term comes to us from Hebrew and basically means "save, we pray." It was a natural part of the shouts of praise and acclaim by the crowd as Jesus rode into Jerusalem on a donkey on that first Palm Sunday (Mark 11:1–10).

The crowds that went before him and that followed him shouted "Hosanna to the Son of David! Blessed is he who comes in the name of the Lord! Hosanna in the highest!" (Matt. 21:9).

Spoken praise to God loses some of its zest, but set praise to music and it has wings. Read the words of Handel's "Hallelujah Chorus" and they are rather mundane. But when a choir sings it you are lifted to the gates of heaven.

The Book of Psalms closes with a chorus of doxologies—Psalms 146 through 150. Here is a plethora of grateful homage in words that deserve to be sung.

See Adoration, Prayer, Thanksgiving.

Prayer

PRAYER is spiritual communion with God. It takes many forms. Those which are the most common and universal are adoration, thanksgiving, praise, confession, petition, and intercession. Each of these is discussed separately in this book. Sometimes our prayers take none of these forms. Instead of "praying," talking to God, we are quiet, listening, waiting to hear the "still small voice." The psalmist captures this mood with, "Be still, then, and know that I am God" (Ps. 46:11). This kind of prayer is called meditation.

Prayers are sometimes individual, sometimes corporate. These are complementary to each other, and both are necessary. Here is an example. My child is sick; of course, I pray for the child's recovery. Then I come to church. There are prayers for the sick in the service; my child is named, along with others who are sick and suffering for whom my fellow worshipers are praying. I also realize that the loving and merciful Heavenly Father is concerned about the sick and suffering around the world. When I go home my prayers can never again be little and selfish. They now embrace all those others who are also the Heavenly Father's concern.

Our private prayers give corporate worship personal meaning. On the other hand, corporate prayer gives our private devotions depth and breadth.

See Adoration, Confession, Intercession, Petition, Praise, Thanksgiving.

Predestination

A belief in PREDESTINATION is the belief that God has determined in advance what will happen to his human children. Through the centuries this belief has been twisted into something very un-Christian: some are predestined to eternal salvation while others are predestined to eternal damnation. This double predestination would turn God into a monster who does not deserve our worship and obedience.

What is the true meaning of predestination?

It is all tied up with the biblical belief about election: God chose the Israelites to be his people. Why them? Why not the civilized Egyptians or the gifted Greeks? We don't know why he selected them, but we do know what being chosen was intended to mean. Those seemingly inconsequential Hebrews were elected to be God's instrument for achieving the salvation of all people (Isa. 49:6). So election means chosen by God for special responsibility, rather than special favor; it means being chosen for mission and service and, along with carrying out these purposes of God, goes the gift of salvation. Jesus in the Gospels makes it clear that Israel failed to carry out the vocation which was theirs by election and it was passed on to the Christian church. The author of the Epistle to the Ephesians writes that "before the foundation of the world . . . he destined us in love" to be his children "through Jesus Christ according to the purpose of his will" (Eph. 1:4–5). We were predestined by God to be loved, loved as his children—persons, not puppets. And as persons we are free to respond to his love, or we can reject his love. In either case, we are responsible for our decision and its results. That is what being a person means: being free to make up our own minds and responsible for the results which flow from our decision.

Do not fall into the trap of thinking that God's foreknowledge of what is going to happen will undercut human freedom and responsibility. God's will and plan is the desire that "all people be saved and come to the knowledge of the truth" (1 Tim. 2:4). Some accept, others reject this opportunity. Whether or not God has foreknowledge of this is a separate issue having to do with the belief about God's omniscience (all-knowingness). Don't let that muddy the waters of our thinking about predestination.

Suppose a childless couple who had always wanted a baby find out that she is pregnant and that they are finally going to have a child. That child-to-be is predestined to be loved. The sad day may come when the youth turns his back on his parents, will have nothing to do with them, and angrily leaves home. But even then he is still loved in spite of the hurt and anguish of his leaving the family. This is what predestination is telling us about God's love for us.

The glorious truth is that God always intended to love all of us, and he always intended that we should be his children, free to respond to his love. And he shows us in the death of Jesus Christ on the Cross what happens, and how much it hurts, when we reject his love.

See Almighty, Creation.

Pride

PRIDE is self-love. Too little of it is unhealthy; too much of it is the root of all evil. Let's take a closer look.

The pride of accomplishment is a necessary ingredient in doing a good job and being a good workman. Self-respect and self-esteem are necessary to good neighborliness; you should love your neighbor as *yourself* (Lev. 19:18; Matt. 22:39). To feel genuinely good about yourself is a healthy thing and becomes a yardstick in genuinely caring about your neighbor.

Pride becomes a dirty word when it is coupled with arrogance, insolence, and boasting. Such an attitude builds a barrier between a person and the neighbor he or she is supposed to love. This kind of self-gratification and self-worship flowers in selfishness which disregards the needs of others. The prophet Ezekiel condemned Sodom and her sister cities because they "had pride, surfeit of food, and prosperous ease, but did not aid the poor and needy" (Ezek. 16:49). Overwhelming pride makes one insensitive and unfeeling.

Jesus warns that those things which come from within a person, "out of the heart of man," as he put it, these are the things which get one in trouble. He cited a long list including evil thoughts, pride, and foolishness. "All these evil things come from within," he concluded, "and they defile a man" (Mark 7:22-23). He listed foolishness along with pride, and rightly so. How foolish it is of me to think that blowing my own horn, looking down on you, and deliberately ignoring your feelings and your needs will enhance my position and make things better for me. Long ago a wise sage put it this way: "Pride goes before destruction and a haughty spirit before a fall" (Prov. 16:18).

See Sin.

Promises of God

THE PROMISES OF GOD are what God has said he will do, and this belief lies behind an appreciation of much biblical thought. Look at the Bible with promise in mind.

The Old Testament has no word for promise, noun or verb, but the idea is there in full blossom. There is the fundamental assumption that a word spoken, especially by God, has the weight of a solemn promise. That is what lies behind the expressions "thus says the Lord" and "the word of the Lord" which occur so often, especially in the prophets. When it is pronounced, it is true, and God keeps his word. It has the force of a solemn promise. When a person of integrity tells you, "I will deliver the goods tomorrow, you have my word," that is a promise; make no mistake. And that is the way it is in the Old Testament, too.

Words of God that especially have the character of promise in the Old Testament are words spoken to Abraham and to David. God gives his word that Abraham will have a posterity as numerous as the stars, and also the gift of the land of Canaan, "flowing with milk and honey" to be Israel's land and the Lord's dwelling place among his people (Gen. 15:5, 18; see also Neh. 9:23). These promises were repeated to Isaac (Gen. 26:3), and to Jacob (Gen. 28:13–14). God's promise to David was that he would always have a descendant on his throne (2 Sam. 7:12, 16).

The promises of God hold a central place in the New Testament as well. The promises made formerly by God to the patriarchs and to the people of Israel are fulfilled in Jesus Christ—"all the promises of God find their Yes in him" (2 Cor. 1:20). With the coming of Christ the time of fulfillment arrived. The prophets had foretold that in the last day the Spirit of the Lord would be shed on every creature (Joel 2:28–29), and the Lord made this a reality at Pentecost (Luke 24:49; Acts 1:4–5; 2:16–21; 32–33).

But ultimate fulfillment lies in the future and Christians are urged to persevere in the faith lest they be cut off from the promise (Heb. 6:11–12; 10:36; 4:1–2). The delayed final fulfillment is in order to give people time to repent (2 Pet. 3:9). But the day will certainly come, and in the meanwhile the gift of the Holy Spirit is an earnest (first installment) of that final consummation (Rom. 8:23; 2 Cor. 1:22; 5:5; Eph. 1:13–14).

The thought forms of the Bible are sometimes difficult for us to assimilate. We are not as moved by God's promise to Abraham or of the idealistic greatness of David's kingdom as were our biblical forebears. The one place where the promises of God have for us the solid ring of reality is in the apostle's words, "All the promises of God find their Yes in Jesus Christ" (2 Cor. 1:20). Not only are the former promises fulfilled in all that he said and did, but he himself was God's promise. Both promise and reality. When he says, "Him who comes to me I will not cast out" (John 6:37), we believe him. That's a promise we find real and hold dear. When he says, "Come to me, all who labor and are heavy laden, and I will give you rest" (Matt. 11:28), we believe him. That promise gives many of us the will to cope and a peace beyond explanation.

In the Old Covenant, Gentiles were excluded from the promise (Eph. 2:12), but in Christ no one is excluded. By baptism we become members of Abraham's posterity, and, consequently, heirs of the promises of God (Gal. 3:26–29). Christians seek to become worthy of the promises already theirs in order to honor the Lord who has granted them these promises (2 Cor. 7:1). So the divine promise is then the foundation of Christians' obedience as well as their hope.

See Covenant.

Prophet

A PROPHET is one of God's spokespersons; but a spokesperson is not a *fortune-teller.* God speaks to people through such individuals.

The great prophets of the Old Testament spoke God's message to the people. God used their minds, their imaginations, their skills, their voices. When they felt sure that God was commanding them to speak, they did so, whatever their message might be. With a total lack of tact they roared out against phoniness and corruption wherever they found it. Amos shocked his hearers by quoting God as saying in effect, "Your fancy, pretty worship makes me sick; it's an abomination! What I want is justice, not sham piety, and righteousness like an ever-flowing stream" (Amos 5:21–24). The priest told him, "Get out of town. Go south of the border. You'll like the bread and you can rant and roar to your heart's content" (Amos 7:12). Two hundred years later the priests in Jerusalem felt the same way about

Jeremiah. Prophets were a terror to kings as well as priests. Nathan told King David to his face that he was a crook and an adulterer (2 Sam. 12:1–15). And so it was with all the prophets.

They did sometimes warn people of what might happen in the future, but their main purpose was to bring God's demand for repentance and reform. To do this they explained the true meaning of things that were happening at the time—an invasion, a famine, injustice in the courts. They were convinced that the Spirit of God gave them their thoughts, told them what to say, and filled them with the courage and power to say it.

The great words of the prophets taught the people, warned them, and gave them hope. In prosperous times, when there was plenty of wealth, they warned people of God's judgment. To people who were proud, conceited, or selfish, they declared that God did not approve of their big houses and expensive clothes; what was important to God was justice, goodness, obedience to him, and a generous concern for the poor. They often said that a dreadful punishment was about to fall upon the nation for its sins. In bad times, when most of the people were poor and worried, the prophets assured them that God had not forgotten them but was willing and able to save them. Sometimes the prophets gave glowing word-pictures of a marvelous time when God would rule the entire earth. Some of them told of the coming of a Great Deliverer, God's Messiah, and of the new, and good things that would happen when he came.

See Promises of God.

Protestant

To be PROTESTANT means standing up for something. The word *protestant*, which is often misunderstood, began its religious history in Germany over four hundred years ago. The authorities of the Roman Catholic church were insisting that the pope and the Church of Rome should continue to have full authority over all Germany. At the Diet of Spiers (1529), men from various parts of Germany stood up and spoke out for their right to religious freedom. These individuals, many of them princes, were admiringly called "protestants" because they had been brave enough to witness to their belief. The word *protestant* basically means "to witness for."

The name came to be applied to the Lutherans in Germany. Later it spread in usage all over Europe, including Great Britain; it came to be used to describe all those who were members of reformed churches and did not give allegiance to the pope.

Protestant and *catholic* are often thought of as opposite terms. They should rather be thought of as complementary, each standing for something the other needs. *Catholic* emphasizes loyalty to the whole Church and its long life down through the ages. *Protestant* emphasizes the fact that the Church is not above being criticized and questioned. Unthinking loyalty turns leaders into bullies and followers into puppets. On the other hand, criticism apart from love and loyalty will undermine and destroy Christian companionship. Each word describes an aspect of church life which should not be ignored.

See Catholic, Church, Witness.

Providence

PROVIDENCE is the Christian belief that affirms God's sovereignty over history and individual lives and his power to fulfill his purpose of love. Strangely, this is at the same time both the simplest and one of the most obscure elements of the Christian faith, central, yet difficult to understand. It is a porcupine belief for it bristles with questions.

The doctrine of providence is a rope with two strands—the lordship and the love of God. God reveals himself as Lord of creation and of history; he also reveals himself as loving his creation and willing its fulfillment. Because he is Lord, God can carry out his will of love in history. The Bible contains many references to his controlling hand in both the world of nature and of individuals (Matt. 6:25–34 and Rom. 8:28–39 are first-class New Testament examples). While this belief finds no place in the Creeds, it crops up repeatedly in our prayers. For instance:

> O God, who by thy providence didst lead our forefathers to this land wherein they found refuge from oppression and freedom to worship thee. . . . (Lutheran: *Service Book and Hymnal*, 224)

> Grant, O Lord, we beseech thee, that the course of this world may be so peaceably ordered by thy providence that thy Church may joy-

fully serve thee in all godly quietness. . . . (Methodist: *Book of Worship*, 139)

O God, whose never-failing providence ordereth all things both in heaven and on earth. . . . (Episcopal: *Book of Common Prayer*, 177)

Among the problems which press for answers in relation to belief in providence are these:

1. How is God's lordship and control of history and events compatible with human freedom and responsibility? Does not belief in providence transform God's children—free to choose between right and wrong, free to love or not—into puppets on a string?
2. We know *we* do wrong things and bad things. Is this the case because we are sinners and chose to behave shamefully and are, therefore, responsible for the mess we've made of things? Or did God pull the wrong strings—and so we couldn't help what we had done and are not responsible?

Our belief in providence tells us that God does not make us sin—we are free to be headstrong and stupid—but he can use even the way we mess things up to fulfill his purposes. As Joseph explained to his brothers, "You meant evil against me; but God meant it for good, to bring it about that many people should be kept alive as they are today" (Gen. 50:20). So it is that many times bad turns out to produce good. To the eyes of faith such happenings are the working of a gracious God. This is what belief in providence is all about. "Nothing will be able to separate us from the love of God in Christ Jesus our Lord" (Rom. 8:33).

God turns the intentions and decisions of our lives to his good purposes in the same way the influence of a great and good person inspires us to reach high; our freedom of decision has not been taken away, but nobler ends are achieved.

See Predestination, Sin.

Purgatory

PURGATORY is a place believed to exist by Roman Catholics and some Anglicans where penitent, dying persons go for a period of temporary, disciplinary punishment before going to Heaven. Practically the only Christians of the West outside the Roman Catholic church who believe in Purgatory are some Anglicans. It is not a biblical belief; rather it is a theological deduction stemming from a belief that the afterlife has two possible ultimate destinations: Heaven and Hell. Purgatory is the place where the saved are punished insofar as they have not received temporal punishment for their sins. There is no teaching as to the nature of the punishment and its duration although the Roman church teaches that souls in Purgatory are profited by the prayers and indulgences of the living.

The Roman Catholic All Souls' Day, November 2, became important in the late Middle Ages when the growing fear of Purgatory brought about dramatic changes in the liturgy. The continental reformers violently opposed the doctrine of Purgatory and masses for the dead.

R

Reconciliation

RECONCILIATION is the act of enabling people to become friends again. Mary and Joan have become estranged because of a misunderstanding and some harsh words. Harriet brings them together, helps them talk out their differences, and rediscover each other as friends. There are tears; there is forgiveness, joy, and warm embraces. This is an example of human reconciliation. While a third person is not always or necessarily involved in bringing about reconciliation, such a go-between is usually present.

In the Bible, *reconciliation* is a New Testament word. The word is not found in the Old Testament, although the idea is there. In Jesus Christ a healing event brought about such a radical change in the situation of people in their relation with God that a new word was needed to describe it. Reconciliation is that word. "While we were enemies we were reconciled to God by the death of his Son," Paul explains (Rom. 5:10).

Reconciliation has a warm sound and a good feeling about it. When you think of two people who mean a lot to you who have become estranged and then have become reconciled, you have a pleasant glow inside. There is something right and wonderful and good about it. Shift this to our relationship with God. Christ who died for our sins and rose again is the Reconciler. We through our littleness, our meanness, and our selfishness shut ourselves away from God's love. Then Christ not only rebuilds that relationship, he makes us his "ambassadors," colleagues in reconciliation. "The world" is brought to God through Christ by reconciliation; and our "ministry," our Christian living, is intended to be a part of that action (2 Cor. 5:18–20). Christ's work and our ministry dovetail.

Reconciliation describes a major way in which we respond to what God in Christ has done for us.

See Atonement, Justification, Mediator, Ministry, Redemption, Salvation, Sin.

Redemption

REDEMPTION is deliverance from sin. Behind this religious word is the idea of buying back. A child is kidnapped and held for ransom. By paying the ransom the child is bought back or delivered from bondage. The New Testament describes what Christ did in dying for us in terms of this kind of transaction—a paid ransom. By his sacrifice he frees us from the bondage of sin. He, therefore, is our deliverer, our redeemer. Here is one New Testament description of this happening:

> You know that you were ransomed from the futile ways inherited from your fathers, not with perishable things such as silver and gold, but with the precious blood of Christ, like that of a lamb without blemish or spot. (1 Peter 1:18-19)

This is the same thing our Lord told the disciples: "The Son of man also came not to be served but to serve, and to give his life a ransom for many" (Mark 10:45). But Jesus never explained in detail what this meant.

You know what it means to redeem a bad check—one for which there are insufficient funds. The necessary money is paid; the bad check is made good. Christian thinkers agree that redemption involves God's gracious saving love in what he did by sending Jesus Christ to give his life for sinful humankind. But they have not agreed as to how he does this. The point at which they do agree however, is that Jesus Christ is the Redeemer, the person through whom our deliverance is brought about. By Christ the Redeemer our salvation is accomplished.

See Atonement, Justification, Reconciliation, Salvation, Sin.

Religion

RELIGION is the way we think and act and live in giving loyalty to God. The word *religion* comes from a Latin word meaning "to tie, to fasten, to bind together." The word *ligaments*, which refers to the tough bands of tissue that hold our skeleton together, has basically the same root. Your religion is what holds your life together. To we Christians, God as revealed in the Bible and in the life of the Church is he who holds our lives together. In him "we live and move and have our being," as Paul told the Athenians (Acts 17:28).

Of the great world religions, two started in India, Hinduism and Buddhism; two began in China, Confucianism and Taoism; one in Japan, Shintoism; one in Persia (Iran), Zoroastrianism; and two started in Arabia, Judaism and Islam. The birthplace of Christianity was Palestine, and it is said to have the largest number of members, more than 500 million. Next in order come Confucianism, Hinduism, and Islam with around 240 million members each.

Only Judaism and Islam are like Christianity in pointing us to a God who is personal and who wants personal companionship with us; who is also the supreme being who controls the whole universe. Christianity is the only religion that has a gospel, a chronological story about the redemption of humanity by God. That redemption is offered to us by God as a gift; it is not earned.

See God, Gospel, Incarnation, Trinity, Worship.

Resurrection

RESURRECTION means rising from the dead.

While Jesus certainly died and was buried, shortly thereafter his faithful followers unquestionably knew him to be alive. Less than a quarter of a century after the crucifixion and Resurrection of Jesus, Paul wrote, "For I delivered to you as of first importance what I also received, that Christ died for our sins in accordance with the Scriptures, that he was buried, that he was raised on the third day in accordance with the Scriptures" (1 Cor. 15:3–4).

Why is the Resurrection "of first importance"? The reason is because it was when the followers of Jesus realized that neither the concerted efforts of human sin (all the evil that brought about his passion and death) nor death itself could conquer him, that they knew beyond question that he was the Son of God. He is known to be "Son of God in power according to the Spirit of holiness *by his resurrection from the dead* [emphasis mine]" (Rom. 1:4), wrote Paul. All of the gospels, written years later, were composed by evangelists who shared this point of view. Their resurrection belief colored all that they wrote about Jesus of Nazareth.

Here are three significant points related to our belief in the Resurrection of Jesus Christ:

1. A part of the importance of the Easter appearances of the Risen Lord is that he was unquestionably the same person whom the disciples had known during his earthly life.

2. After the Lord's Ascension, experiences of his risen presence were different, but nonetheless real. The Apostle Peter, who was a primary witness of the Lord's Resurrection, wrote shortly before his own death, "Christ died for sins once for all, the righteous for the unrighteous, that he might bring us to God, being put to death in the flesh but made *alive in the spirit* [emphasis mine]" (1 Pet. 3:18). So it was that the presence of the Risen Lord was a firsthand experience for believers who were not able to share in the Easter appearances.

3. The account of the Risen Lord appearing to two disciples on the road to Emmaus (Luke 24:13–35) shows us two important ways in which Christians of the ages and we ourselves experience his risen presence. "Did not our hearts burn within us . . . while he opened to us the Scriptures?" they said. Then, when they returned to Jerusalem their excited report to the assembled disciples was that "he was known to them in the breaking of the bread." These are our experiences also. We too are often aware of his presence among us when in the course of our worship we hear the Scriptures read and explained. And when we share in the Lord's Supper—"the breaking of the bread"—his risen presence is again awesomely real.

See Almighty.

Resurrection of the Body

THE RESURRECTION OF THE BODY is the belief that beyond the grave we shall be whole and complete persons. Each of us is made up of body, mind, and spirit. The whole of it is what makes me ME. The phrase "resurrection of the body" in the Apostles' Creed means that we believe that when we are redeemed and raised from the dead, we will be wholly ourselves. God provided us with a body so that we could live in this world. We are confident that he will provide us with a body which will be suitable for our life in the world to come—"the body which is to be" (1 Cor. 15:37).

There is another dimension to this tenet of faith. Because of my body, I am an accountable, responsible person. H. G. Wells once wrote a story about a man who drank some concoction and became invisible. Since no one could see him, no one could catch him if he did something bad. Because of my body I am identifiably me. I am accountable; I must accept responsibility for what I say and do. To believe in the resurrection of the body is to believe that beyond the grave I will be identifiable, and I will be accountable.

What we do in this life has eternal dimensions. We never cease being responsible persons in the sight of God.

See Immortality.

Revelation

REVELATION is that knowledge which comes to us from God, not something we found out on our own. The Bible is the record of how God disclosed himself to people through the years. He did it gradually, not all at once; it is the way in which we get to know people in our own lives. Suppose through happenstance you and a distant relative in England begin corresponding. You are complete strangers, but because of the letters that person begins to be more of a friend. Suppose he or she happens to visit this country and you receive a telephone call. Think how much better you know that person now. His or her tone of voice reveals the real person better than words on paper could. Finally, that relative comes to see you. Then you really get acquainted.

Somewhat similarly God reveals himself to people over a number of centuries. The Bible shows God acting in history. He created everything. He freed the Israelites from slavery in Egypt. By this act he made himself known to Israel as a people (read Psalm 105). He later showed himself through the words of the prophets who were his spokesmen. Finally, he came to us in a person, the man named Jesus of Nazareth. "The Word became flesh and dwelt among us" (John 1:14). God revealed himself supremely in Jesus Christ, his work, his life, death, Resurrection, Ascension, and the promise of his coming again. This is the high point of God's personal revelation of himself to us.

See Incarnation.

Reverence

REVERENCE is a feeling of deep respect tinged with awe; it is our attitude toward God. If you meet a friend on the street, you probably just say, "Hi." If you should be invited to meet the president of the local college or a justice of the Supreme Court, you would be more respectful. If you met the president of the United States or the British prime minister or the pope, you would hardly know what to say; you would be overwhelmed. One thing is certain: you would not be chatty or flip.

Then you come into the house of the Lord. You hear, or the hallowed surroundings cause you to sense, that "the Lord is in his holy temple, let all the earth keep silence before him" (Hab. 2:20). You are in the presence of the Lord of lords, the *Almighty*. And you seem to hear a celestial herald saying,

> Holy, holy, holy, is the Lord God Almighty,
> Who was and is and is to come. (Rev. 4:8)

You are speechless. You can only bow down and worship. An ancient sage put it this way:

> Guard your steps when you go to the house of God. . . . Be not rash with your mouth, nor let your heart be hasty to utter a word before God, for God is in heaven and you upon earth; therefore, let your words be few. (Eccles. 5:1–2)

This is what reverence means.

See Almighty.

Righteousness

RIGHTEOUSNESS has a double meaning. There is an ordinary use of the word and a more profound religious use. Both are found in the Bible. Both were used by Jesus.

The everyday, street-corner use of the word *righteousness* means right dealings, acceptable conduct by some agreed standard. Jesus uses the word in this sense to refer to those who were faithful to the practices of Jewish religious life. "I have not come to call the righteous, but sinners to repentance," he said (Luke 5:32).

The other use of the term stems from the fact that God is the source of uprightness or morality. "No one is good but God alone," Jesus reminds us (Mark 10:18). We human beings are sinners; we have not obeyed his righteous will. Only God can put us in the right with himself. That is what the word *justify* means. In his Parable of the Pharisee and the Tax-Collector Worshiping in the Temple, Jesus says of the tax-collector, "This man went down to his house justified [put in the right with God] rather than the other" (Luke 18:14). This meaning of righteousness has deep Old Testament roots:

1. The psalmist, knowing himself to be a sinner, addresses God, the righteous King-Judge: "Hear my prayer, O Lord; . . . answer me in thy righteousness. Enter not into judgment with thy servant; for no man living is righteous before thee" (Ps. 143:1–2).

2. The petitioner knows that mercy and goodness are the stuff of which God's righteousness is made: "In thy righteousness bring me out of trouble! In thy steadfast love, cut off my enemies" (Ps. 143:11–12).

3. Now the humble worshiper prays that the King-Judge will lift him up and assist him to live better: "Teach me the way I should go, for to thee I lift up my soul. . . . Teach me to do thy will, for thou art my God!" (Ps. 143:8, 10).

God is the righteous One and man, the sinner, can only come into a right relationship with him through repentance and putting his faith in the merciful goodness of the King-Judge. Therefore our attitude toward the righteous God is a blend of trepidation and confidence (Mic. 7:9).

Righteousness as used in the epistles is always the righteousness of God in this Old Testament sense. To Paul the good news of Jesus Christ is that through his death and Resurrection God the King-Judge has pronounced a verdict which has entirely altered the condition of human beings towards him. In Jesus' death the righteousness of God is revealed and is appropriated by believers; "He who through faith is righteous shall live" (Rom. 1:17).

The Christian is put in the right with God through faith in Jesus Christ and not by doing good things in an effort to win God's favor. To Christians, right behavior, right dealings, and good works are done out of gratitude for what God in Christ has done for us. They are not a way to win God's favor; only repentance and faith can accomplish that.

See Justification, Sin.

Ritual

A RITUAL is the prescribed routine of worship. Without some sort of ritual there could be no organized method in religious worship. The services of our churches' prayer books are rituals. The distinctive thing about these rituals is that they are not solo performances; more than one person must take part. Those who gather for a service come together, or congregate, to share in a ritual which is conducted by a minister or priest or celebrant, and the participants expect to receive some grace or blessing as a result of participating. The congregation is a necessary part of the proceedings and their participation in the ritual tends to make the body of worshipers one. Such is the nature of a liturgical service.

A particular ritual is usually referred to as a *rite*.

S

Sacrament

A SACRAMENT is the name given by Christians to a rite or ceremony regarded as an instrument through which God bestows his grace or unmerited favor on the faithful participants. More commonly, this is described as an outward and visible sign of an inward and spiritual grace.

With the exception of the Society of Friends (the Quakers) all Christians accept baptism and the Lord's Supper as sacraments ordained by Christ (Matt. 28:19; 1 Cor. 11:23–26). The Roman Catholic church and the Orthodox churches of the East have five other sacraments—confirmation, penance, extreme unction, holy orders, and marriage. The Reformation churches and the Anglican churches only recognize the two sacraments specifically ordained by Christ (though some Anglican worshipers recognize all seven); they consider the latter five sacramental rites. They contend that Christ did not command their observance and they do not consider inferences from the words of Scripture, though supported by ecclesiastical tradition, sufficient evidence to give them sacramental status.

A sacrament is always twofold. In holy baptism water, the sign of the cross, and, in some cases, anointing with the consecrated oil of chrism are the outward sign. The inward grace is that the candidate becomes a member of Christ, a child of God, and an inheritor of the Kingdom of Heaven. What is seen is a washing; what is experienced is an adoption into the Family of God. In the Lord's Supper what is seen is a feeding: participants are given consecrated bread and wine. These become vehicles of God's grace whereby through faith communicants receive the Body and Blood of Jesus Christ for the strengthening and refreshing of their souls.

The sacraments are the "means of grace" through which God bestows his unmerited favor and strengthening power upon those who come to him in faith.

See Baptism, Confirmation, Eucharist, Grace, Matrimony, Ordination, Penitence, Unction.

Sacrifice

A SACRIFICE is something valuable which is offered up or given away. The practice of sacrifice is as ancient as a pre-biblical times tribe that gives a human sacrifice to placate the gods, and as modern as this morning—parents who give up much so that their child may go to college. It is as serious as the act of the soldier who dies trying to save his comrade on the battlefield—the "supreme sacrifice," and as frivolous as a sacrifice hit in a baseball game which advances a runner. Sacrifice is a universal practice which can have deep religious meaning.

Sacrifice as a religious rite was performed in Old Testament times for several reasons. Sometimes it was a food offering intended to nourish God—the showbread in the Tabernacle (1 Sam. 21:1-6). Then there was the sacrifice of firstfruits (Exod. 34:26). God has rightful claim on all the products of the soil and only after he has been given the firstfruits is the remainder deconsecrated, so to speak, and available for use in common life.

The Old Testament sacrifice for sin was usually a blood sacrifice. An animal was killed, its blood was poured out and its flesh offered up on the altar, a sort of ransom paid to God in order that sinners might be reconciled to him. Because of the sins of old Eli's sons, God tells the boy Samuel that "the iniquity of Eli's house shall not be expiated by sacrifice or offering" (1 Sam. 3:14). The Old Testament concept reaches its most profound view of sacrifice in the description of the role of the Suffering Servant of the Lord:

> Surely he has borne our griefs
> and carried our sorrows;
> yet we esteemed him stricken
> smitten by God, and afflicted.
> But he was wounded for our transgressions,
> he was bruised for our iniquities;
> upon him was the chastisement that made us whole,
> and with his stripes we are healed. (Isa. 53:4-6)

This is vicarious sacrifice—suffering willingly accepted on behalf of others.

Jesus saw himself in this role. The heavenly voice at his baptism—"Thou art my beloved Son; with thee I am well pleased" (Luke 3:22)—is in part quoting directly from an earlier Servant poem in that second Isaiah sequence (Isa. 42:1). And the Gospel writers could find no words better to describe his passion than those quoted above.

In the Eucharist, we are caught up in his sacrifice, forgiven, and reconciled to God. That is why it is called "Eucharist" which means thanksgiving. Moreover, we are fed and strengthened by his life and Spirit that we may go forth in gratitude to live lives filled with loving acts of self-sacrifice for others.

See Atonement, Eucharist, Salvation, Sin, Suffering Servant.

Sadducees

SADDUCEES were members of a conservative sect within ancient Jewish society. In their literal interpretation of Scriptures they rejected the oral laws and traditions dear to the Pharisees. They denied belief in the afterlife because it is not mentioned in the Pentateuch (the first five books of the Old Testament); body and soul are mortal and both cease to exist at death (see Luke 20:27–40).

The word *Sadducees* means "descendants of the priest Zadok" (1 Kings 2:35; 1 Chron. 29:22), who according to Ezekiel (40:46; 48:11) alone had the right of officiating in the temple. They were a party of priests, the superior sacerdotal caste, as well as aristocrats who supported them.

In politics the Sadducees collaborated with the ruling power (in New Testament times, the Romans) which in turn protected them. They constituted a majority of the members of the Sanhedrin, the supreme legislative and highest ecclesiastical and secular tribunal of the Jews.

See Pharisees.

Salvation

SALVATION is that mighty act of God which he wrought for humankind by sending his Son into the world. By this divine graciousness we human beings are delivered from our sinfulness into new life of wonderful fulness. Because of our sin—our arrogant insistence on being our own god—we are estranged not only from God, but also from our fellow humans. Moreover, we are victims of a tumult within ourselves—lonely, guilt-ridden, ashamed.

"For us and for our salvation," God's Son "came down from heaven . . . and was made man." So states the Nicene Creed. After Christ's death and Resurrection, New Testament writers began trying to explain the wonderful thing he had done. Their efforts, and those of theologians down to this present, have resulted in a cluster of metaphors.

- By his death Christ saved us from the consequences of our sins. (*Salvation*)
- What he did for us atoned for our sins and brought about our "at-one-ment" with God. (*Atonement*)
- His death was a ransom paid in order to redeem us. (*Redemption*)
- By his death he put us in a right relationship with God; that is, he justified us. (*Justification*)
- In Christ God brought about our reconciliation with himself. (*Reconciliation*)

All of these and others are various facets of the same glorious truth: Salvation is of Christ the Lord. Through our faith in Jesus Christ, crucified and risen, we have been forgiven and made God's children by adoption and grace. We have been saved from the powers of evil which dominate our lives.

This does not mean that we have been removed to some safe place in existence where danger and temptation cannot overtake us. Rather it means that we have an unexpected and undeserved power to stand firm and not be shaken in the midst of danger.

A young man with a wife and baby is having a hard time making ends meet. In his job he handles company money. Taking a little of it would certainly make life easier for his family. He talks the situation over with a friend who says, "No, don't do it. I believe in you and your boss believes in you." And then he adds, "I have temptations too. That is a reason why I go to church. Somehow I have the feeling that Jesus believes in me, and I don't want to let him down; and he gives me strength not to."

Such a person knows what it is to be saved. The temptation is still there, but the strength to resist it is also present. Jesus Christ is the Savior; he brings salvation to those who are open to receive it, and who put their trust in him. In his great hymn, "A Mighty Fortress Is Our God," Martin Luther proclaims this profound realization: "Did we in our own strength confide / Our striving would be losing." And he couples with it the conviction that it is Christ Jesus who "must win the battle" for us.

Jesus was talking about salvation when he said, "I am come that they might have life and have it abundantly" (John 10:10). That wonderfulness is only the half of it. This abundant life has the everlasting qualities of life with God, this side of the grave and beyond.

See Atonement, Faith, The Fall, Justification, Reconciliation, Redemption, Sin.

Sanctify

SANCTIFY means to make holy, to set someone or something apart for God's special purpose. Only the Holy Spirit can make us holy. God does not force himself upon us, however. We are free to refuse the influence of the Holy Spirit. God begins the work of making us holy when we are baptized, but we must be willing to have it happen. We must let the Holy Spirit work within us to help us. Through the Spirit we become mature men and women, measured by Christ as a standard (Eph. 4:11–16).

Not only do we pray that the Holy Spirit will sanctify our lives, but we ask that he will sanctify those things which are used for sacred purposes in our worship. We ask God to sanctify the water used for baptism, the bread and wine used in the Eucharist, and to sanctify us so that as a result of receiving the Sacrament we may serve him faithfully.

The Holy Spirit works to sanctify us through the Church's sacraments, through other people, through Christian groups to which we belong. He always works to bring our plans and actions into agreement with God's holy will.

See Baptism, Grace, Holy Spirit, Saint.

Schism

SCHISM is what happens when a group of church members strongly disagree with the larger body: they split. *Schism* comes from the

Greek word which means exactly that, "to split." A schism is usually a formal division within, or a separation from a church over some doctrinal belief. Here is one early example: The Baptists separated from the Church of Rome because they believed that infant baptism was wrong, that people should be able to decide about being baptized for themselves; they should be baptized as adults just as Jesus was. They were first called "Anabaptists," re-baptizers. Their break with Rome was a schism (about A.D. 1520).

See Baptism.

Sin

SIN is separation from God stemming from disobedience. It is the exaggerated self-esteem that enables us to substitute our will for God's will, our purposes for his purposes, our desires for his desires. In a word, we become God's rivals, rather than his children. In the Garden of Eden story the serpent succeeds in tempting Eve to eat the fruit that God had commanded her not to eat with the words, "You will not die [as God warned that you would]. For God knows that when you eat of it your eyes will be opened, and *you will be like God* [emphasis mine], knowing good and evil" (Gen. 3:4–5). That is when the fruit became irresistible: "You will be like God." Sin is revolt against the King of the realm, it is not a minor transgression such as walking on the grass or driving over thirty miles an hour.

Sin is referred to as separation from God, for that is what happens. When we quarrel with a friend, we may be in the same room with him or her, but we are still separate in a very real sense.

There is a difference between *sin* and *sins*. *Sin* is our basic disposition to run our lives as we want to, not as God's loving and faithful children. *Sins* are the unpleasant ways in which we demonstrate this. We are arrogant, proud, selfish, grasping, impatient, and all the rest. All the negative things we are doing are saying to the world, "I'm first," "I'm best," "I count the most," "I'll do it my way." This kind of behavior is the very opposite of the attitude expressed in the prayer our Lord taught his faithful followers to pray: "Our Father, who are in Heaven, hallowed by thy Name, thy kingdom come, thy will be done on earth as it is in Heaven."

This leads us to the concept of *original sin*. An easy definition of original sin is that it is a taint which all people inherit from the disobedience (i.e., the Fall) of Adam and Eve in eating the forbidden fruit. Rather let us think of it as a universal infection which results from undue self-regard. A baby's earliest experiences confirm a sinful view of the world. For when mother enters the nursery she goes directly to the crib; obviously the child is at the center of things. When the baby is brought into a family gathering everyone makes a fuss over him or her. The baby is, of course, the center of attention. Will not that baby conclude that he or she is the center of importance in the world? While it is true that as the child grows he or she will be taught to share and to be unselfish and considerate, there is something which militates against such commendable behavior. Paul explains that there is something originally in us that is foreign to being a faithful child of God. "I do not understand my actions," he writes. "For I do not do what I want, but I do the very thing I hate." He seems to be amazed at this discovery about himself. It is not "the good I want, but the evil I do not want is what I do" (Rom. 7:15, 19).

Sin is also corporate. Communities sin, nations sin. Communities sin by permitting slums to exist or in failing to protect children from the drug traffic at schools. States and the nation sin when developers are permitted to denude countrysides of trees thus causing terrible floods, or when they do not provide low-cost housing for the less affluent, or when there is no regulation of manufacturing so as to prevent the scourge of acid rain which kills vegetation (and perhaps, people). Nations sin when they devalue human life or run roughshod over neighboring countries. Undoubtedly the prophet had our corporate sins in mind as well as our individual transgressions when he said: "All we like sheep have gone astray; we have turned everyone to his own way; and the Lord has laid on him the iniquity of us all" (Isa. 53:6).

Our Christian life is not just abstaining from doing bad things; it is also, and more importantly, trying in every way to do good things. But often we deliberately avoid a plain duty; we think of a kind act we ought to do and then just don't do it. That is sinful. But this is not all; we do things we know we should not do. God has shown us his holy will. We have the Ten Commandments and our Lord's teachings in the Gospels. We hear and can know our duty. But by our willful choice we decide to do what we please. We set up a "Kingdom of Me" in place of the Kingdom of God. We let our lives be ruled by "Me," not God. So we act proudly, claiming to run the show.

Such is the nature of sin.

Soul

THE SOUL is one way the New Testament describes a person in relation to God. It is not a separate and distinct part of a human being which can be taken out and analyzed. In the New Testament a person is only and always seen as he or she stands before God—the whole individual. This is hard for us to comprehend in this scientific age when we dissect everything and psychoanalyze anything we cannot put under a microscope. The New Testament talks a lot about "the body" and also has a great deal to say about "the soul," but it *never* speaks of "body and soul" as though they were two different parts of a whole human being. Two photographs of a person, a front view and a profile, are not pictures of separate parts that can be removed from the rest of the body and analyzed in isolation. They are different views of the same whole person. So it is with body and soul; it is the same individual in his entirety viewed from a different angle.

The *body* is that corporal bulk which is essential to human existence. The nature of a human being is most obviously expressed in his or her physical body. Body equals the human person in his or her entirety. If you want to be a human being you have to have a body. First you will need a physical body to live on this earth, then you will need a spiritual body in order to carry on in the hereafter. Paul spells this out in 1 Corinthians 15:35–44.

The *soul* is an aspect of this same human being from another point of view. This is a person in his or her character as a living being. The soul is human life regarded as the life of an individual being with consciousness and will. "Now is my soul troubled," said Jesus as he contemplated his coming Passion (John 12:27). Often English translations of the Bible use *life* in the place of the word *soul*. For example, "for what will it profit a man, if he gains the whole world and forfeits his *life*? Or what shall man give in return for his *life* [emphasis mine]?" (Matt. 16:26).

Adam became a living soul when God breathed into his nostrils the breath of life. That is why *soul* and *life* and *spirit* are used almost interchangeably.

See Resurrection of the Body.

Steward/Stewardship

A STEWARD is a person who manages property which belongs to someone else. The title occurs frequently in our Lord's parables (Matt. 20:8; Luke 12:41–43). A steward is a caretaker. The New Testament use of the term goes beyond the idea of taking care of another person's property. The Christian steward is to manage *God's* property faithfully and well. That property consists of one's abilities— "As each has received a gift, employ it for one another, as good stewards of God's varied grace" (1 Pet. 4:10). It also includes a person's money— "All things come of thee, O Lord, and of thine own have we given thee" (1 Chron. 29:14). Of course, we cannot exercise this stewardship without realizing it includes a dedicated management of our allotted threescore years and ten, the time God has given us in this world.

A Christian *stewardship*, then, is the proper use of his time, talents, and money for the glory of God. Many conscientious Christians have found ways to give of their time and talents in the service of the Lord—doctors, lawyers, carpenters, agriculturalists and anthropologists in Third World countries, teachers, . . . the list is endless. And the stewardship of our money recalls us to the biblical standard of tithing—one-tenth is owed to the Lord (Mal. 3:8, 10). This means that one's giving is not in terms of an amount but in terms of a percentage.

At a time when the Christians in Jerusalem were in great need Paul wrote to the members of the Church in Corinth telling them of the giving of their Macedonian brethren and urging them to follow that example. His appeal is the longest passage in the New Testament on the subject (2 Cor. 8:1–9:15). It throws light on the Christian stewardship of our money.

Suffering

SUFFERING simply means "to bear." We bear pain but we don't like it and we're baffled as to why we should have this unpleasantness.

The Bible is full of this universal experience. There is hardly a page on which suffering is not mentioned. The supreme example of suffering is that of the Passion of our Lord. (*Passion* in this case means "suffering" rather than strong emotional or sexual desire.) Here is an indelible picture of the wrongness which stalks creation and at the same time of the redeeming love of God.

We usually think of suffering in terms of physical pain. But often suffering is emotional, not physical; it is caused by scorn, maliciousness, desolation, being the victim of the hard-heartedness of others. The Bible goes beyond even this: suffering is more than physical or emotional evil. It has a spiritual character: it seems to be a sign of God's rejection. This is hard for us to accept, but even our Lord in his suffering on the Cross turned to a psalm which depicts divine rejection—"My God, my God, why hast thou forsaken me?"—instead of some sturdy psalm of trust, such as Psalm 91. Unexpectedly, the opposite of suffering is not health and well-being; rather it is consolation (2 Cor. 1:5-7) and glory (Rom. 8:18). In other words, by God's grace we have the assurance of God's favor *even though we may still suffer.*

In the Bible, suffering is linked to the sinful condition of humanity, and this explains why, as Jesus said, "the Son of man must suffer many things" (Mark 8:31). For the Son of God really to become a full human being "he had to be made like his brethren in every respect"—that is, like us in suffering as well as in being tempted. Only thus could he be our Savior (Heb. 2:14-18). This is why the suffering of Jesus Christ, the Servant of God and the Son of man, lies at the very heart of the message of the New Testament. Paul makes it clear that the suffering of believers is linked to that of their Lord, and that suffering freely accepted enables us to share the destiny of our Lord who through suffering entered into glory. "If we suffer with him, we shall also be glorified with him" (Rom. 8:17), he says.

So the sum of the matter is that the Christian looks upon his or her suffering in this world as a sharing in Christ's suffering and, consequently, considers it a pledge that in the world to come he or she shall also share in Christ's glory. Therefore, "rejoice in so far as you share Christ's suffering, that you may also rejoice and be glad when his glory is revealed" (1 Pet. 4:13).

See Incarnation.

Suffering Servant

THE SUFFERING SERVANT OF THE LORD is the name applied to the individual who is the subject of a series of poems in the Book of Isaiah. There are four of these poems which describe the servant of the Lord: Isaiah 42:1–9; 49:1–7; 50:4–11; and 52:13–53:12. The servant is pictured in these poems as patiently suffering for the sins of others in order to bring them back to their intended place as God's faithful, loving children.

Scholars disagree as to (1) whether the author has a particular individual in mind, such as the Prophet Jeremiah; or (2) whether he is thinking of the servant's role as that of Israel, the chosen people; or (3) whether he is describing the role of the messiah who is to come. In any case, Jesus saw himself as fulfilling this role. The gospel writers were aware of such striking parallels between the Lord's Passion and the Isaiah descriptions that their accounts of Jesus' trial and Crucifixion are filled with Isaiah quotations.

Sunday

SUNDAY is the Lord's day; a time for worship and rest. The keeping of one day of the week as a non-working day is very ancient and has long been a custom among many types of religious people including Jews, Christians, and Moslems. The story of the Creation in Genesis tells us that even God rested after he made the world. That is why Jews observe the seventh day of the week, as one of the Ten Commandments clearly explains. The Jews think of Saturday, or the *Sabbath* as they call it, as a time to rest from everyday work, indoors and out, and also as a special holy day on which to remember the partnership between God and his people. It is a day of rejoicing in the Lord.

Christians, however, have a new reason for rejoicing: Christ has risen from the dead. This changes not only their lives but also their calendars. It was on Sunday, the first day of the week, that women came to the tomb and learned that Jesus had risen from the dead. This was the wonderful new event by means of which God in Jesus Christ showed himself victor over sin and death. So Christians celebrate the day of Resurrection every week on Sunday and every year on Easter.

At first Christians observed both the seventh day and the first day of each week. Gradually, however, the observance of the Sabbath dropped out of Christian observance as the keeping of the Lord's Day became more and more important. Each Sunday was a "little Easter," and we still celebrate it as such: "O God, you make us glad with the weekly remembrance of the glorious Resurrection of your Son, our Lord" as one prayer puts it. For a long time the Greek name for *Sunday* meant "the day of Resurrection." Quakers still call it "First Day."

Our Sunday is a day of joy and worship, and it also provides a time for rest, a change of schedule, and family recreation. By setting aside one day particularly for churchgoing, rest, and recreation, we remind ourselves that life has a meaning not seen on the surface and that God stands at the center of our daily decisions. Also we gain new physical and spiritual energy to live our lives better.

See Worship.

Symbol

A SYMBOL is something that is used to represent something else. A Christian symbol is a sign or object which stands for an important fact about God and brings it home to us.

If you saw a picture of a cut-down cherry tree and a hatchet and were asked what it stood for, you would say, "For George Washington when he was a boy." This is a symbol, because there is no picture of young George in it. It is the fallen tree and the hatchet that bring the story to your mind. In the same way the highway sign showing a child running is a caution that there are children in the neighborhood; it means, drive carefully. When you know what a symbol means you can "read" it in less time than it takes to read the words that would have to be used in its place.

For centuries people have agreed that a cross stands for Jesus Christ or Christianity, crossed keys for the Apostle Peter, a chalice for the Lord's Supper, a dove for the Holy Spirit, and sea shell for Baptism, and so on.

Some symbols, like hatchets and road signs, are symbols established by humans. The crossed keys, cross, chalice, dove, and sea shell are also humanly derived symbols which are helpful to us because they bring important ideas about the Christian faith into our minds. But the water in baptism and the bread and wine in the Lord's Supper are divinely given symbols. They not only tell us something, or put an idea into our heads, they also *convey* something. The Church expresses this by saying that they are "effective signs"; they *do* the very thing that they symbolize. So water, which symbolizes cleansing, does actually become the vehicle for cleansing us from our sins when it is used in holy baptism. And bread and wine, which symbolize nourishment, do actually bring us the presence of Christ and strengthen us with his life when we receive them in the Lord's Supper.

See Sacrament.

T

Thanksgiving

THANKSGIVING is that form of prayer in which we express our gratitude to God. As the prayer of adoration involves loving God for himself, the prayer of thanksgiving involves thanking him for what he does.

This is perhaps the place where all prayer should begin: listing all the good things in one's life for which you know you are not responsible and thanking God for them. Count your blessings on your knees. You cannot thank God too often for even the lowliest of blessings.

A person for whom praying had become perfunctory and meaningless sought the help of a wise and godly counselor. "For the next ten days," he suggested, "why don't you just thank God for your many blessings—friends, family, love, health, work to do, and all the rest." Counting your blessings is a well-trod road into the presence of God.

Even adversity may in retrospect be recognized as a blessing. Vandals broke off the radio antenna on my car. Since I was about to drive through the mountains for a speaking engagement and wanted the radio for the trip, I took the car in to be repaired. The mechanic informed me that my brakes were dangerously worn. He fixed the antenna, and after repairing the brakes he said, "You would never have made it safely through the mountains."

> Praise the Lord, O my soul,
> and forget not all his benefits, . . .
> Who saveth thy life from destruction,
> and crowneth thee with mercy and loving-kindness.
> (*Book of Common Prayer*, p. 466)

See Prayer.

Transfiguration

THE TRANSFIGURATION OF CHRIST is that pivotal incident in the Gospels in which Peter, James, and John recognized Jesus as the Messiah, the fulfillment of their religious heritage (Matt. 17:1-8; Mark 9:2-8; Luke 9:28-36).

The week before, Peter had put the disciples' growing conviction into words – that Jesus was the long-expected Messiah (Christ) and Jesus had immediately begun telling them that "the Son of man must suffer" (Luke 9:18-22). They were still wrestling with these big, new ideas – that their Jesus was the Christ and that the Christ must suffer – when Jesus took his intimate three disciples up a mountainside for a time of prayer. In the early morning light they saw Jesus transfigured, a "dazzling white raiment" (Luke 9:29), talking with Moses and Elijah – symbols of their heritage, the Law and the prophets – and a heavenly voice said to them, "This is my Son, my Chosen; listen to him!" Shortly thereafter the Old Testament personages disappeared and the disciples were alone with Jesus whom they now knew to be not only God's Son but also the fulfillment of all that the Law and the prophets meant.

Transubstantiation

TRANSUBSTANTIATION is the belief that in the Eucharist the bread and wine actually become the Body and Blood of Christ. The Roman Catholic Council of Trent (1545) defined this doctrine as "that wonderful and singular conversion of the whole substance of the bread into His Body and of the wine into His Blood . . . the species [that is, the outward appearance] only of the bread and wine remaining."

Consubstantiation is another belief as to what takes place when bread and wine are consecrated during the Lord's Supper or Holy Eucharist. According to this belief the substance of the Body and Blood of Christ are said to coexist in and with the substance of the bread and wine.

These are two of the ways in which theologians seek to explain the holy mystery of how God spiritually strengthens and refreshes those who come to his table in faith.

See Eucharist, Consecration.

Trinity

THE HOLY TRINITY is the belief in one God who makes himself known to us as Father, Son, and Holy Spirit. The word *trinity* means "three-in-one." There are three Persons—God the Father, God the Son, and God the Holy Spirit—but we worship only one God. How can this be? A mystery. Our little, finite minds can never encompass the fullness of the infinite God.

The Holy Trinity is difficult to comprehend, no matter what one's age or education. Perhaps an analogy will help. Take the story of a book. It first exists in the mind of an author. No one can see it, but it is very real even though the author has not yet put it down on paper. Then he or she writes the book and it is published. It becomes something everyone can see, handle, examine, read. The day of publication is its birthday. Then one day it ceases to be published and circulated; it goes out of print. But it continues to have an influence. It is quoted and appears in footnotes long after it ceases to be available. This is the story of one book, but it has had three manifestations, each different, each real.

In a way this helps us appreciate the mystery of the Holy Trinity. The triune God depicted in the creeds has three manifestations. He is God the Father, Creator of heaven and earth—unseen but very real. He is God the Son, Jesus Christ our Lord—he came into history at a definite time, he lived, suffered, died, and he is remembered to have said, "He who has seen me has seen the Father" (John 14:9). He is God the Holy Spirit—the Spirit that inspires the Church and her members is like the Jesus of Nazareth whom the disciples knew. The Spirit, said Jesus, "will glorify me, for he will take what is mine and declare it to you" (John 16:14).

See Creed, God, Holy Spirit, Jesus.

U

Unction of the Sick

UNCTION OF THE SICK describes the Church's ministry of healing. Jesus told his disciples to heal the sick. They often did this, anointing them with oil (Mark 6:13). James says that if we are sick, we are to ask the elders to anoint us (Jas. 5:14–16). He also advises us to confess our sins. The reason is that if we have sins on our conscience and keep them locked up inside of us, they may make our sickness worse. The sensible thing is to make a clean breast of it and receive absolution. Then when the priest or minister anoints us with oil or lays hands on us in blessing, our Lord's power can heal us, body and soul. Of course, we should also obey the doctor; unction is intended to bless his work, not to take its place.

V

Vestments

VESTMENTS are the church attire worn during the conducting of worship. The first vestments in Western Christendom were principally the formal secular dress of the Roman Empire of the early centuries of the Christian era. In time there were garments specifically designed for liturgical use as distinct from the reservation of one's "best clothes" for such a purpose. As the use of vestments continued there was the tendency to try to find a biblical rationale for them in terms of details of the Passion, and to interpret them in terms of a symbolism of virtues and graces.

This special church clothing serves several useful purposes.

1. It should be beautiful for it is the very essence of worship that it should reflect and acknowledge the beauty of God as revealed in his mighty acts of creation and redemption.
2. It serves a historical and theological function. The vestments are ancient in origin and reflect the continuity of Christian worship through the ages.
3. Finally, vestments are functional. They enable worshipers to be able to distinguish the roles of each participant.

Priests have several eucharistic vestments:

THE CASSOCK is a long (usually) black garment which reaches to the feet. Actually it is not really a vestment but is worn under the vestments; it is used as street attire.

THE ALB is a long white garment with narrow sleeves which is worn over the cassock. It is appropriate as a symbol of purity and wholeness acquired by the Christian in baptism.

THE AMICE is a broad band of white material, sometimes ornamented with embroidery, which is worn about the neck. It was originally a protection for the head and neck against the cold; later it came to symbolize the helmet of salvation.

THE MANIPLE originally was a towel or napkin, worn on the left forearm just as a waiter does. It symbolizes the humility which befits a servant of God.

THE STOLE is a long narrow scarf, usually of silk, which hangs about the shoulders and symbolizes the yoke of service. Its color is usually that of the church season and it is decorated with appropriate symbols.

THE CHASUBLE is a large garment which is put over the head, and hangs down in front and back. Both front and back may be marked with Y-shaped crosses or orphreys, ornamental designs. The *orphrey* in front is sometimes a single strip or pillar and is said to represent the column or pillar to which our Lord was bound. This vestment may be white or the color of the church season and it is frequently ornamented with embroideries. It is said to represent the seamless coat with which our Lord was clothed, and signifies love.

In some churches the priest or minister wears a cassock, surplice, and stole for celebrating the Holy Eucharist instead of eucharistic vestments.

THE SURPLICE is a flowing vestment of white material which is worn over the cassock. It is a modified version of the alb and, like the alb, reminds us of the purity of life which should characterize those who minister in the sanctuary.

In some Protestant churches the minister wears an academic gown and sometimes an academic hood. Still other Protestant ministers prefer to preside in civilian dress. The latter are actually returning to the very early Church practice of reserving one's "best clothes" for the conduct of public worship.

Vigil

A VIGIL is wakefulness and watching during the normal hours of sleep. In the life of the Church a nocturnal, devotional watching is part of the preparation for the observance of a great festival. The Great Vigil of Easter has been a practice in the Church since at least the second century, and probably earlier. It consists of readings which bring to mind the pivotal events of our Old and New Testament heritage, and instruction. In ancient times, those who had been instructed during Lent were baptized at dawn, the bishop laid his hands on them, and they joined in the first Easter celebration of the Eucharist.

See Church Year.

Virgin Birth

THE VIRGIN BIRTH refers to the birth of Jesus from Mary his mother while she was still a virgin. The principal account from which the Lord's virginal conception comes is the Annunciation. The angel Gabriel appeared to Mary telling her that she was to have a Son who would be the Son of God and that she was to call his name Jesus (Luke 1:26–38).

Whether the source materials which Luke had before him as he wrote his Gospel represent the Church's attempt to express the great significance of Jesus or whether a historic event lies behind the words is not known. Unquestionably Matthew believed in the virginal conception of Jesus (Matt. 1:18–25) and Luke seems to have believed in it, although he limits his view to two gentle references (Luke 1:34; 3:23). At the same time he does not hesitate to call Joseph Jesus' parent (Luke 2:33, 41, 43, 48) and have Gabriel proclaim that Jesus will have "the throne of his father David," a messianic identity in part proven by his lineal descent from David through Joseph (Luke 3:23; see also 18:38; 20:41). The problem here is that Luke is striving to express the ineffable in human terms. It is not surprising that human language breaks down under the strain and recourse is made to the language of symbolism.

Those who believe the Virgin Birth is simple history must believe that the story came ultimately from Mary herself—a beautiful, awesome, treasured part of Christian heritage. But there are others who find this belief hard to accept. To support this latter view is the fact that neither Mark, in the earliest Gospel, nor Paul, whose Epistles antedate the Gospels, make any reference to it. Paul unquestionably believed in the divinity of Christ (Rom. 1:3–4), and Mark's Gospel is about "Jesus Christ the Son of God" (Mark 1:1). Either they did not know about the Virgin Birth or they did not think it was important. The fact is that the story does not seem to have influenced early Christian thinking about Jesus. This would suggest that it was not known because it was not developed until a later date.

The Annunciation in Luke is that evangelist's view, based on tradition of how the birth of Jesus is to be understood. The account shrouds the event in mystery but one thing is clear: the Son of Mary is the Son of God, the long-promised Messiah.

Let it be recognized that the pivotal Christian belief is the Resurrection of our Lord, not the Virgin Birth. From the earliest moments of Christian preaching and writing, Jesus Christ the Lord has been recognized as "Son of God in power according to the Spirit of holiness *by his Resurrection from the dead* [emphasis mine]" (Rom. 1:4). So whether the Virgin Birth is fact or symbol it remains a precious and beautiful part of the heritage of all who believe in the Risen Lord. We are indebted to Luke for the story of the Annunciation, which—like raindrops on a rose—is to be viewed with appreciation, not subjected to the rough hands of angry argument.

Vocation

OUR VOCATION is what God has called us to do with our life, so it is sometimes referred to as our *calling*. Our vocation has two aspects: (1) what we are able to do with the abilities and aptitudes which God has given us, and (2) what will enable us to be fellow workers with God, helping make this world a better place for his children to live in.

Sometimes it takes a little doing to find out what our special gifts are. For surgeons and musicians and teachers and other similarly fortunate people whose God-given abilities have been trained and whetted and who enjoy what they are doing, vocation and job blend into one. But for a host of others, this may not be so. The work one has to do in order to eat may just bring in money and often seems to have no dimension of being God's calling. But it may depend on the attitude of the individual.

There was once a clerk who spent her days behind a counter receiving people's monthly payments to an electric power company. Dull, unimaginative work. But she talked to them, listened to the family stories of their ups and downs, and remembered. On their recurring visits she would ask, "How is your Mother?" "Did your dog recover from being hit by that car?" "Has your daughter found a job yet?" She was the bright spot in their day, perhaps in their month—a warm ray of caring in a dark, cold world. God had given her a big, warm heart and she used it to his glory. That is what vocation is.

The dean of the Washington Cathedral stopped one day to talk with laborers who were helping lay a new sewer line in the cathedral close. "What are you getting out of this?" he asked one of them. The man looked puzzled as though it was obvious. "A bit more than the minimum wage," he replied. A bit later, the dean asked another man the same question. Looking up at the towering stone magnificence, he replied, "I'm building a cathedral!" Tennessee Williams, the playwright, once said, "Lots of us are in the gutter, but some of us are looking at the stars."

It is those who are looking at the stars who have discovered the meaning of vocation for themselves, and are making the world a better place in which to live.

See Ministry.

W X Y Z

Witness

A WITNESS is one who tells the truth that he or she knows from his or her own experience concerning some person or event. The truth that a witness tells is called *evidence* or *testimony*. For example, a witness in court takes an oath and promises to tell all he or she knows about something. Perhaps the person saw an automobile accident and can say, "I was standing on the corner and saw a car coming down the street, and then suddenly it turned sharply to the left." As a witness, he or she gives information based on personal experience. Witnesses tell what they think they saw, what they believe is true.

The Greek word for witness gives us our word *martyr*. People who tell the truth at the cost of their lives are martyrs. In the early days of Christianity there were followers of Jesus Christ who gave witness to their faith in our Lord by accepting death rather than deny him and pretend that they were not Christians. They were bearing witness by deeds as well as words.

Everyone who stands up for Christ and his teaching is a witness for him. As Peter said to Cornelius, the Roman officer, "We are witnesses to all that he [Jesus] did" (Acts 10:39). Every Christian by virtue of his or her baptism is intended to be a witness for Jesus Christ. In the Episcopal service, this is made explicit. The candidate is asked, "Will you proclaim by word and example the good news of God in Christ?" And the candidate replies, "I will, with God's help."

All Christians make their witness to Jesus Christ in their everyday places of living – home, neighborhood, on the bus, in the shop or school or office, at picnics, in community gatherings, everywhere they meet and rub shoulders with other people. What they say and think and do is observed by others. We bear witness, often without realizing it, to what we think about justice and right, about compassion and concern for the poor and disadvantaged, about our respect for the dignity of other people, about our commitment to God and his Church. It is not so much what we *say*, rather it is what we *are* that makes a lasting impression on those around us. No one could be in the presence of Martin Luther King, Jr., very long without realizing that one had been in the presence of a champion of justice and a man of God. "What you *are* speaks so loud I cannot hear what you *say*," someone once said; that is what Christian witness means.

During the weeks following the Lord's resurrection and ascension Peter and John were often addressing crowds of people on Jerusalem street corners, and saying, "Know assuredly that God has made him both Lord and Christ, this Jesus whom you crucified" (Acts 2:36). That kind of talk would stir up trouble, so the religious authorities had them arrested. At the trial the judges wondered at the boldness and courage of Peter and John and "recognized that they had been with Jesus" (Acts 4:13). That is what Christian witness is for everyone of us: something about us makes people realize that we have been with Jesus.

See Mission.

The Word

THE WORD is a mixture of something heard and something observed. We experience this fact in daily life as well as in the Bible. Words reveal what you are like: *"I love you." "I hate you." "I forgive you."* Words can also convey a person's authority and power. When we try to understand the meaning of the Word of God and of simply the Word, we discover, beyond its ordinary meanings, profounder and grander ones.

The Word is the essential way in which God relates to the world. It was by his Word that he created the heavens and the earth (John 1:1–2).

It was through his Word that he revealed himself to humankind: Jesus Christ was the Word made flesh. And it was through proclaiming him to the world that the history of the Church developed and is fulfilled (Acts 4:29, 31). The whole story of salvation to which Scripture bears witness is the Word which God addresses to the world. Let us examine this.

In the Bible, the Word is partly verbal expression – something heard. But when the prophets said, "Thus says the Lord," the Word of God was more than a message, it was an encounter. Their hearers were brought face to face with the living God. The Word of God was not impersonal, general wisdom, rather because of it, hearers were instructed and confronted and challenged. Those who had ears to hear were sometimes smitten and humbled, sometimes awed and uplifted. Through his spoken Word, God had become present to them and had touched their lives.

But the Word of God is considerably more than just verbal expression; it enters history, charged with explosive power; it is an event. "My word . . . goes forth from my mouth . . . it shall accomplish that which I purpose, and prosper in the thing for which I sent it" (Isa. 55:11). The Word of God created the world, stirs up the elements (Ps. 147:15–18), controls them (Matt. 8:24–27), says to the paralytic, "Rise and walk," forgives sins (Matt. 9:1–8), and so on.

Throughout the Bible, the Word has this double aspect—an element of knowledge and an element of power.

The supreme revelation of the Word of God is Jesus Christ. All that the Word means in the Old Testament becomes flesh and dwells among us (John 1:1–14). The words of Jesus demand faith in him who pronounces them. They do not refer to some general truth, but to Jesus' person. The words and actions of Jesus are inseparable. "In him," wrote Paul years later, "all the fulness of God was pleased to dwell" (Col. 1:19). He is the Word.

In the days following the Lord's Resurrection and Ascension, the apostles preached the Word. They were not recalling and declaring the words of Jesus, but rather they proclaimed Jesus himself, for to preach the Word is to preach Jesus Christ. Moreover, their preaching was accomplished by demonstrations of the Spirit and of power (1 Cor. 2:4). Miracles, brotherly love, forgiveness, practiced and received—in brief, the life of the Christ, was then and always has been a preaching of the Word.

See Incarnation, Bible.

Worship

WORSHIP is giving honor and homage to God; originally the word was *worthship*.

It is easy to worship a false god without really meaning to. For one's "god" is that which has the supreme place in one's life and receives loyalty and devotion. My "god" is the unifying, motivating force around which my life is built. For some, money is that most important something. "I will do it for you, if you will pay me." How much he or she paid for a coat or a car is of major importance, and if one can find a bargain or cut a corner and save a few dollars, that is great good news. To another, the most important thing may be the opinion of others. Everything he or she says or does is with an eye to what others may think, with its value being measured by others' thoughts. Or one's god may be success, power, influence, or any of a host of other false deities. Our god is whatever we give the supreme "worthship" to, for that is what worship means.

Our Christian God is the God and Father of our Lord Jesus Christ. The Bible helps us know how to worship him in sincerity and truth.

From earliest times people have set aside a day to come together for public worship. The first creation story concludes with: "God rested the seventh day from all the work which he had done. So God blessed the seventh day and hallowed it" (Gen. 2:2-3). Therefore, setting aside the seventh day as holy found its way into the Commandments and became a day of public worship. The seventh day is the Jewish Sabbath. In time Christians changed to the first day of the week because of the Lord's Resurrection. But the point is that on a regular day people stopped everything and consciously came into God's presence. They worshipped him whom they knew to be their Maker, Redeemer, Sustainer, and Friend.

Coming together for worship is the primary way in which we are related to God. We are members of his Family, the Church, and therefore know him as our Father. It is in being together that we know the Spirit of the Family, that is, the Holy Spirit. (This is also true of our human families; with no coming together, there is no family spirit.) And it is the Spirit which teaches us how to pray (Rom. 8:26-27). Also it is in being together for worship that we rub shoulders with our neighbors whom we learn to love as brothers and sisters. In the process we discover that it is in loving them that we learn to love God (1 John 4:20-21). It is in caring about them and forgiving them that we receive forgiveness ourselves (Matt. 5:14-15). It is in coming to the Lord's Table with them that we have a foretaste of the heavenly banquet and are sustained by that holy food which enables us to serve as his faithful children in our daily pursuits.

Regular public worship is not an option; it is a Christian necessity.

It is true that the worship of God can take place anywhere, at anytime. The fact is, *it doesn't*. Unless there is a regular time and a regular place for public worship, it will not occur. No one ever took his golf clubs to the golf course in order to pray. Anything worth doing has to have a time set aside for it, and Christians set aside Sunday for worship.

We express our deep feelings of God's supreme importance when we come together to worship, and we do this through singing, through hearing the Word read and explained, through ancient and modern prayers, through the breaking of bread, and through some prescribed ritual, part of it perhaps as ancient as the Church itself and part of it as contemporary as the morning newspaper. Then, having recalled ourselves to the truth that God stands at the center of our lives and of our universe, we go forth to bear witness to his power and love in our daily pursuits as butchers and bakers and candlestick makers.

See Holy Spirit, Idolatry, Prayer, Religion, Reverence, Sunday.

BIBLIOGRAPHY

Jones, Cheslyn, Wainwright, Geoffrey, Yarnold, Edward, S. J., eds. *The Study of Liturgy,* New York: Oxford University Press, 1978.

Lutheran Book of Worship, Minneapolis: Augsburg Publishing House, 1978.

Ordo Lectionum Missae, Vaticana, Rome: Libreria Editrice, 1969.

Service Book and Hymnal, Minneapolis: Augsburg Publishing House, 1958.

The Book of Common Prayer, New York: Church Hymnal Corporation, 1979.

The Book of Worship for Church and Home, Nashville: The United Methodist Publishing House, 1964.

The Church Year—Calendar and Lectionary, Minneapolis: Augsburg Publishing House, 1973.

The Hymnal 1982, New York: The Church Hymnal Corporation, 1985.

The Interpreter's Bible, 12 volumes, New York: Abingdon Press, 1957.

The Worshipbook—Services and Hymns, Philadelphia: The Westminster Press, 1970.

Thomas, Owen C., *Introduction to Theology,* Cambridge, Mass.: Greeno, Hadden & Co., Ltd., 1973.

Von Allmen, ed., *A Companion to the Bible,* New York: Oxford University Press, 1958.

INDEX